A Guide to Nature in Winter

A Guide
to Nature in Winter

Northeast and North Central
North America

DONALD W. STOKES

Illustrated by
Deborah Prince and the author

Little, Brown and Company — Boston — Toronto

A

LIBRARY OF CONGRESS CATALOGING IN PUBLICATION DATA

Stokes, Donald W
  A guide to nature in winter.

  Bibliography: p.
  Includes index.
  1. Natural history—North America. 2. Winter—North America. 3. Nature study. I. Title.
QH102.S76   574.5'0974   76-26861
ISBN 0-316-81720-1
                                   E

MV

Designed by Susan Windheim
Published simultaneously in Canada
by Little, Brown & Company (Canada) Limited
PRINTED IN THE UNITED STATES OF AMERICA

How to Use This Book

This book contains a number of separate field guides, one for each prominent aspect of nature in winter. Each guide is divided into three parts: general information on the subject, a key for identifying the different members of the subject, and specific natural history descriptions of each of the members.

The general information will be most useful if you read it before going out, for it will most likely expand your conception of winter and sharpen your approach to seeing.

The keys are designed for simple use in the field, but becoming familiar with them ahead of time will make it easier for you to identify things when you find them.

After identifying a plant or animal, look up its name in the natural history description that follows the key; the names are in alphabetical order. These descriptions point out things to look for and enjoy in what you have found. If it is too cold to read them in the field, remember the name and read the description later in the warmth of your home.

Contents

A Guide to Nature in Winter

I

Winter Weeds

*M*OST PEOPLE THINK weeds are particularly offensive types of plant, when in reality many plants we call weeds are used in other countries as cash crops or garden ornaments. There is really no difference between plants and weeds; weeds are simply plants growing where they are not wanted.

But despite the fact that weediness is in the eye of the beholder, there are certain plants which continually grow where not wanted, and they all have at least three features in common. First, they are aggressive colonizers, either producing great quantities of seeds that are widely dispersed or having far-reaching roots which produce new shoots. Second, they grow primarily on land affected by humans, such as cleared or cultivated land, roadsides, gardens, and dumps, and in this land they can tolerate a wide range of soil and climatic conditions. And third, most of these plants, now widespread in North America, are not native to this continent, but were brought here from Europe by early settlers, either knowingly as herbs, or accidentally, as in livestock feed or in the ballast of ships.

When these plants were introduced, the northeastern quarter of North America was dominated by an established forest. The new weeds could not have survived in that damp environment of filtered light, competing with plants already well adapted. But when the settlers cleared land for towns, farms, and roads, a new environment was created, one filled with sunlight and turned-over earth. This was the aliens' previous haunt and they quickly dominated it, spreading by way of roads and paths, from town to farm and from town to town. A few native plants have learned to compete with them, but to this day the alien weeds stick close to humans, shunning the dark forest and crowding into the sunlight and often poor soil of roadsides, fields, and vacant city lots.

Some of these plants remain standing throughout winter, and these can be called winter weeds. One of the functions of these dried weeds is to disperse seeds. Two methods of seed dispersal are most common. One is by wind, as in Milkweed, where seeds are supported on the air by an attached parachute of filaments. The other is by animals, as in Burdock, where the seeds are encased by burs, which get caught in the fur of passing animals. These two methods are seen repeatedly among winter weeds, each species having its own variation on the theme.

Although most weeds in winter appear dried and lifeless, this is far from the case. Some are, indeed, completely dead except for seeds at the tips of their stalks (e.g., Wild Lettuce, Peppergrass); but others are still alive, either within the ground as strong roots (e.g., Dock, Cattail) or above as living deciduous stalks (e.g., Spiraea).

To get the most from hunting and observing winter weeds you need to be aware of all their points of interest, including their life patterns, their use by animals, their adaptations for survival, their method of seed dispersal, and of course the beauty of their colors and forms.

Not all winter weeds are included in this guide. Only those that are particularly longlasting, beautiful, or interesting appear here. These can be found in any open space, from city lots to roadsides to wild meadows. In fact, this is one aspect of nature that may be actually more diverse in the city than the country.

Key to Winter Weeds

For each winter weed there is a drawing of its silhouette and, next to it, an enlarged drawing of a portion of its flowerhead. The average height is given below the name. In order to facilitate identification, most of the drawings are grouped under headings suggesting outstanding characteristics.

WEEDS WITH THORNS OR BURS

Thistle
2–4 ft.

Burdock
3–6 ft.

WEEDS WITH TRANSLUCENT "SEEDPODS"

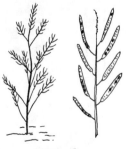 

Mustard
1–3 ft.

Peppergrass
1–2 ft.

WEEDS WITH NO BRANCHING

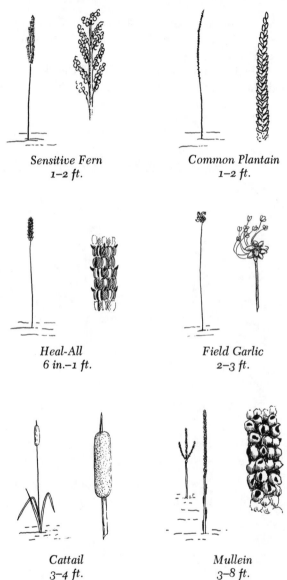

Sensitive Fern
1–2 ft.

Common Plantain
1–2 ft.

Heal-All
6 in.–1 ft.

Field Garlic
2–3 ft.

Cattail
3–4 ft.

Mullein
3–8 ft.

WEEDS WITH BRANCHING ONLY AT TOP

Yarrow
1–2 ft.

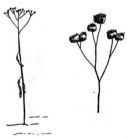

Tansy
2–4 ft.

Joe-Pye Weed
2–4 ft.

Bulrush
2–4 ft.

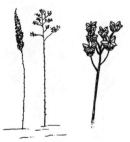

Spiraea
2–4 ft.

Goldenrod
2–4 ft.

WEEDS WITH OPPOSED BRANCHING

Teasel
3–5 ft.

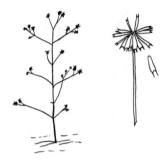

Beggar-ticks
2–5 ft.

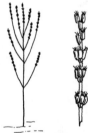

Loosestrife
3–5 ft.

Motherwort
2–4 ft.

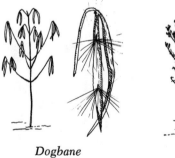

Dogbane
1–3 ft.

St. Johnswort
1–2 ft.

WEEDS WITH SPARSE BRANCHING ALONG THE STEM

Aster
1–2 ft.

Black-eyed Susan
1–3 ft.

Chicory
2–3 ft.

Wild Carrot
2–3 ft.

Milkweed
2–4 ft.

Evening Primrose
2–4 ft.

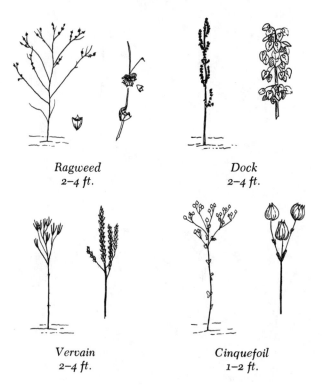

Ragweed
2–4 ft.

Dock
2–4 ft.

Vervain
2–4 ft.

Cinquefoil
1–2 ft.

Natural History Descriptions

Asters (*Aster* species)

Asters are typically the flowers of fall. Their name, which means "star," is derived either from their bright petaled blossoms or the star-shaped pattern of their tiny winter flowerheads. These dried flower parts are similar to those of Goldenrod, another winter weed, and reveal the close relationship between the two plants.

Aster

Both are members of the famous family of Composites, considered one of the most modern and successful products of plant evolution. Instead of producing large petals to attract insects, Composite flowers are individually small and inconspicuous, but they grow in groups, forming a showy mass. The plant conserves energy by producing fewer petals. And it is more efficient for pollination, for one insect can pollinate hundreds of tiny flowers in a single visit.

There are over 250 species of Asters, some of which last as winter weeds. Asters are perennials and their underground roots remain for many years, producing new flowers each fall. So, having found Asters once, you will know where to find them again, both in winter as a dried stalk and in the next fall as a blossoming plant.

Beggar-ticks (*Bidens* species)

It is likely that Beggar-ticks will find you before you find them. After a winter walk through lowland fields you can expect your socks, pants, or coat to be covered with its small seeds. The Latin name of the genus means "having two teeth," but knowing Latin won't help avoid the consequences. Each seed is covered with a hard coat which has at least two barbs covered with backward-directed hairs like the points of a harpoon. The seeds are arranged on the winter stalk with these barbs projecting outward. Since the seeds are loosely attached, the slightest contact with fur or clothes insures their transportation to a new area. Beggar-ticks are annuals, and must be replanted every year. So each plant you find is from a seed carried and dropped in that place last year.

From left to right, seeds are: Beggar-ticks, Spanish Needles, Swamp Beggar-ticks, Leafy-bracted Beggar-ticks

The plant favors moist ground, as found in swamps or ditches. Its large, bright yellow summer flower, a welcome addition to these unused wet areas, has earned it the additional name of Brook Sunflower.

Its other common names are more descriptive of its winter habits: Spanish Needles, Sticktights, Bur-Marigold.

There are a number of species of *Bidens* in North America. Each has a slightly different seed shape or number of attached barbs, but all are the same in their habits. Next time you get stuck with Beggar-ticks you might as well relax and enjoy it. Pluck out a seed, compare it with the ones shown here, and see what kind has found you.

Black-eyed Susan

Black-eyed Susan (*Rudbeckia* species)

The flower of Black-eyed Susan is truly the "day's eye" (the original meaning of Daisy) of summer meadows, a black center surrounded by bright yellow petals staring up from among the grasses. But in winter only a few clues lead us to a remembrance of that summer quality, and one is the black-eyed center, now a marvelous design of matured seeds. The seeds are arranged in spirals, descending both clockwise and counterclockwise from the top of the cone. Their crisscrossing geometry is somehow startling, reminding us that the mathematics of our minds has long been present in nature.

Hard to distinguish from Black-eyed Susan in winter is its close relative, Coneflower, so named because of its dark

*Black-eyed Susan
flowerhead*

cone-shaped center. Both plants belong to the genus *Rud-beckia*, a name given by Linnaeus in honor of his botany professor, Olaf Rudbeck (1660–1740), a man who also once wrote a book claiming Sweden to be the site of the lost Atlantis.

The species named for Black-eyed Susan, *Hirta*, means hairy, and refers to hairs that cover the leaves and stem. They probably protect the plant from losing too much water through evaporation.

Black-eyed Susan is a biennial, forming just a rosette the first year. It loves to grow in hot sunny fields and is a native of our midwestern plains. As more and more people migrated to the Midwest and roads were cut through the wilderness, Black-eyed Susans moved east. Now in the East and South they are a common sight, enlivening fields and roadsides with their sunny presence.

Bulrush (*Scirpus* species)

The Bulrushes form a large group of similarly shaped grasses. A number of them are conspicuous in winter, and

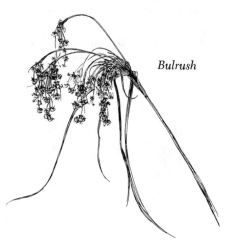

Bulrush

their lone stalks, topped with a fountain of flower parts and seeds, will be found by even the most casual winter weed collector. They are picturesque plants and make a fine addition to any winter weed arrangement. They always grow near water — sometimes in it, sometimes at its edge, sometimes set back in a marshy area. In this moist soft earth they easily extend their rootstalks, which in turn send up new shoots.

Bulrushes are extremely valuable to wildlife. Waterfowl feast on the dark seeds; Muskrats enjoy the rootstalks. They also provide cover for nesting birds and young mammals.

Most Bulrushes are distinguished from other grasses by their triangular stems, but those most often found as winter weeds have round stems. Other common names for members of the genus *Scirpus* are Woolgrass and Threesquare.

Burdock (*Arctium* species)

Finding your clothes studded with Burdock's burs can be an irritating discovery. But it is also a chance to learn at first hand about the animal dispersion of th plant's seeds. You have obviously been chosen as a likely volunteer to perform the job.

The efficiency of Burdock's seed dispersal is due to the structural design of the bur. Its outside is covered with

Burdock bur

small recurved hooks, which easily penetrate fur or clothing but, once in, hold the bur tight. Attached to the hooks are sheaths, which enclose the seeds. When an animal pulls on the bur the hooks lock, so that the sheaths separate, thus releasing the seeds. The fact that Burdock is a native of Europe and Asia, and now widespread in North America, is proof enough of the success of its method.

Burdock is a biennial. It takes two years to flower and produce seeds, completing its life cycle. In the first year it is

Burdock first-year rosette

a rosette of foot-long leaves; during the second summer it grows a tall stalk with pink flowers which later in the fall form burs.

There are two main species of Burdock in North America: Great Burdock (*Arctium lappa*), which grows a stalk up to ten feet tall, and Common Burdock (*Arctium minus*), which grows to only half that height.

At the end of the first year's growth, Burdock's large taproot qualifies as an edible winter vegetable; it has also been harvested commercially for medicinal purposes. The second-year summer stalk is also edible when peeled and boiled. As food for wildlife, however, Burdock is seldom used, because the seeds are well protected by burs, the stem is lined with

Burdock

tough fibers, and the large leaves contain an extremely bitter juice.

Cattails (*Typha* species)

Cattails are a sign of an environment in transition, for they are a key plant in changing wet areas into dry land.

Cattails

Growing in the shallows of ponds and swamps, their starchy rootstocks form a thick mat just under the water surface. Each year as old stalks die back, new shoots grow from the root stalks. In a few years the marshy area around the roots may become covered with decaying matter from earlier growth. This creates soil where once there was water. Plants that prefer this moist earth move in, crowding out the Cattails. Meanwhile, the Cattails produce new shoots, farther out in open water. In this way Cattails and their companion plants continually encroach upon the open water of ponds and swamps.

This succession can be slowed by the presence of Muskrats, which use Cattails for all aspects of their lives. They eat the shoots in spring, the leaves and stems in summer, the roots throughout the fall and winter. Besides using the dense stands as protective cover, they use the stalks and leaves to construct their water homes. Cattails also provide protective cover for nesting wildfowl.

Cattail flowerhead

The brown, cigar-shaped flowerheads topping the tall stems contain up to 125,000 seeds per head, surrounded by packed fluffy matter. All through winter these flowerheads continue to break apart, looking like the stuffing from leaks in old chairs, while wind and water carry the seeds to new muddy areas of the shoreline. In winter the fluff is used by mice to insulate their homes, and in spring it will be used by birds in the lining of their nests.

Cattails are easily seen while driving, for they grow well in the moist drainage ditches that line highways, their rigid stalks and velvet brown seeds firm against the winter wind, lasting until midsummer.

Chicory (*Cichorium intybus*)

Look for the fine grooves that run the length of Chicory's winter stalk, giving it a delicate tooled appearance when viewed from close up. The flowerheads that were bright blue and daisylike in summer, now dry, hug the main stems in groups of two's and three's. Inside some of them you will see the flat ends of wedge-shaped seeds arranged in a circular pattern. If none are visible, then the seeds have been shaken out already by the wind.

Chicory flowerheads

Chicory stalk

On the lower stem are remains of Chicory's small leaves. A second type of leaf grows at the base in summer and is

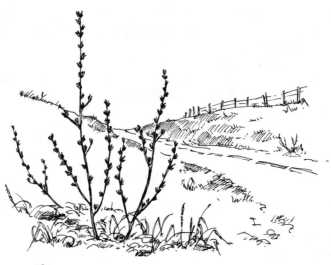

Chicory

the reason for Chicory's fame. Both Chicory and its cousin Endive (*Cichorium endiva*) grow scallop-edged basal leaves that for centuries have been used as salad greens. Even more of a delicacy are the blanched leaves of Chicory. To grow these you must dig out the roots in fall, bury them in a box of soil, and place them in a dark warm area. With watering, the roots produce white or light yellow leaves which make a crisp addition to any salad. This accounts for one of Chicory's common names, Witloof, or "white leaf."

In the southern United States and many countries of Europe, Chicory is grown as a commercial crop for its long taproots. When roasted and ground up, these make a strong additive to, and sometimes a hardy substitute for, coffee.

Chicory is a native of Europe, brought to North America by European immigrants who were accustomed to using it. It is a perennial and thus takes a few years to become well-established; nevertheless, it is extremely common. It is found in the neglected edges of parks, sidewalks, and roadsides.

Cinquefoil (*Potentilla* species)

Cinquefoil is a weed that is common in open areas with poor soil. It rarely grows more than knee-high and has lovely open branching. At the tips of each branch there are cup-shaped flowerheads, which now loosely contain numerous small seeds. As you knock the plant in passing, the seeds are shaken out through the open edges of the cups.

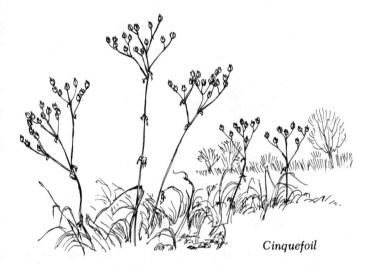

Cinquefoil

There are many species of Cinquefoil, some low-lying plants, others erect and shrubby. The one most often found in winter is Rough-fruited Cinquefoil. Like other Cinquefoils, it sends out leafy runners across barren ground. At various points these runners send down roots and produce a

Cinquefoil flowerheads

vertical stalk. The stalk dies back in winter, but very often the runner remains green. This system of vegetative reproduction is similar to that of rootstocks but occurs above the ground and is thus well suited to colonizing rocky impenetrable soil.

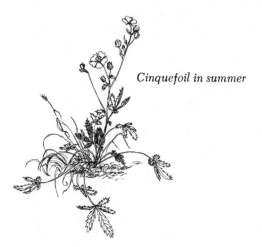

Cinquefoil in summer

The common name, Cinquefoil, means "five leaves" and describes the five serrated palmate leaves. They resemble a miniaturized version of the leaves of Horse-chestnut. The generic name is derived from the Latin word for "powerful"; it was given in the belief that Cinquefoils were valuable as an astringent medicine. There seems to be no present evidence of this healing power, although the roots of some species are edible, and a tea can be made from the leaves of another.

Common Plantain (*Plantago major*)

To get a close look at Common Plantain, bring a stalk inside, for it's too delicate a job for gloved hands or numbed

Common Plantain

fingers. You may find Plantain in your own backyard, or along a well-worn path through a field, but never where the vegetation is tall or thick, for it cannot compete with other weeds. It does best where other plants are cut back regularly, as in a yard; one of its common names is Dooryard Plantain.

Another common name for it is Rattail, which describes its long pointed stalk coated with seed capsules at the tip. Look closely at the capsules and see the tiny cap that covers each one. You can gently pull this capsule off the stalk and break it into two perfect halves, thus releasing the seeds. There are about fifteen seeds in each capsule and hundreds

Common Plantain flowerhead

of capsules on each stalk. The seeds, being slightly sticky, are dispersed by birds and mammals.

When the seed germinates in spring it grows into a rosette of large, rounded, dark green leaves. In the second year, the plant produces the stalk with seeds, and since it is a perennial, it produces seeds each year thereafter. The seeds are eaten by birds and mice; rabbits favor the leaves and stalks. Some species of Plantain can be used as spring greens, and the dried leaves of others make a fine tea.

Although not particularly beautiful, Common Plantain has a likable character all its own, being the only winter weed that is so slender, pointed, and unbranched, reaching from the edges of park paths and growing peacefully at the base of the back doorstep.

Dock (*Rumex* species)

Dock is one of the most striking winter weeds to be found; its rich red-brown color, its spiked clusters of seeds, its gently curving stem, all combine to give it an air of abundance and vitality in the winter landscape.

It is a member of the Buckwheat Family and has the

Dock

Dock seeds   *Dock winter rosette*

characteristic triangular seed. Each seed is enclosed by
three heart-shaped leaves folded in upon it. The seeds have
a faint but pleasant taste and have been used to make flour,
but it is more work than the taste is worth. Dock has
evolved protective coatings around its seeds, so when they
are eaten by some animals, they are not digested but dispersed in the animal's feces. This is a common property of
many weed seeds and an important mode of dispersal.

Dock is a perennial, sending up new leaves each fall in
the form of a rosette. These can be gathered in winter by
digging through the snow at the base of the winter stalk.
They are long lance-shaped leaves which, when boiled and
seasoned with butter and salt, make a fine vegetable, rich in
vitamins C and A. Some prefer Dock to our cultivated spin-
ach.

In the loose soil of your garden, Dock can grow a taproot
up to six feet long, and if you cut off the leaves this root just
sends up new shoots. So the way you view Dock just depends on your state of mind; it can be either a tenacious
weed or a source of healthful food and winter beauty.

Dogbane (*Apocynum* species)

Immediately conspicuous on Dogbane are its silk-parachuted seeds, smaller than those of Milkweed, yet clearly similar to them. Its pencil-thin pods grow in pairs off the plant and split down their inner seams to release seeds. All parts of the plant are thin and gangly, so that it has a slightly untidy appearance.

Dogbane flowerhead and seeds

If you peel the reddish bark from the branches or stem you will find it tough. It was used by American Indians to make twine, and the plant's common name, Indian Hemp, reflects this custom.

The summer leaves of Dogbane have long been known to be poisonous (the word *bane* means poison or death), and, interestingly enough, tropical members of the same genus also contain potent poisons. Many of these poisons are used on the tips of arrows and spears, enabling hunters to capture game more efficiently. But there is nothing to fear of our Dogbane in winter; there are only its color and form to enjoy and its silken seeds to release in the wind.

Evening Primrose (*Oenothera biennis*)

The winter fruits of Evening Primrose are one of its loveliest aspects. Almond-shaped, they split into four sections at their

Evening Primrose seedcases

unattached end, curling back like the petals of a woody flower. Each of the four sections is lined with two rows of loose seeds; they look like coffee grounds, being brown and irregularly shaped. Occasionally insect larvae will spend the winter in these cases. (Obviously any structure the plant produces to contain its seeds will make a fine winter home for insects. Many other fruits of winter weeds are used in this way.)

The name Evening Primrose comes from the plant's curious summer habits. The yellow flowers open usually at night and may be pollinated by a night-flying Sphinx moth. The moth hovers like a hummingbird in front of the flower, unrolling its long tube-mouth to suck the nectar. Each plant opens only a few flowers at any time.

Evening Primrose in its first year is a tight rosette of lance-shaped leaves. The roots of this rosette are a fine vegetable and, in fact, for best eating should be collected in winter. Just look for the new leaves near the base of a winter stalk

Evening Primrose
winter rosette

and dig up the attached root. Boil the roots twice if they taste too peppery; then salt and butter them. Starting with the second spring, the root becomes woody and the plant produces the large stalk that lasts through the winter.

Field Garlic (*Allium vineale*)

Shooting up from among grasses of winter meadows is Field Garlic, its tall lone stem topped with a tangle of dried flowers. Where there is one plant, there are usually others scattered nearby.

Field Garlic spreads primarily by two methods of vegetative reproduction. It grows from bulbs similar in appearance to fresh garlic bought at a supermarket. These bulbs produce new adjacent bulbs, which eventually split off and grow shoots of their own. Garlic's other method of reproduction occurs at the tips of the stalks. Instead of flowers, it

Garlic bulb

more commonly produces a tight cluster of small bulblike growths called "bulbets." These become hard, and throughout the winter they drop off the tip of the stalk, quickly growing into new plants in spring.

There are many plants in the same genus as Garlic — e.g., Wild Leek, Wild Onion, and Chives — all with similar physical characteristics: growth from bulbs, narrow leaves with parallel veins, and six-part flowers. The bulbs and bulbets of

Field Garlic bulbets

some varieties of Garlic are sweet and tender, but others, especially Field Garlic, are far too strong for us to eat. Even the slightest taste will stay on your breath for the day, regardless of efforts to cover or remove it. Perverse as it may seem, cows and livestock love this strong flavor and will eat Field Garlic whenever they can lay their mouths on it. Since it will flavor the animals' meat or milk, farmers try to avoid this situation, for although there may be some demand for garlic beef, there is no market for garlic milk.

Goldenrod (*Solidago* species)

On the winter stalks of Goldenrod look for round or elliptical swellings about halfway up the stem. These are a com-

Goldenrod with galls

mon natural phenomenon known as "galls." Insects form them in summer by laying eggs inside young stems. With the eggs there is a chemical which causes the plant to form a tumorous growth around the eggs. When the eggs hatch, larvae use this growth for food and, after maturing, often winter over in the space they have hollowed out.

Three types of Goldenrod galls are commonly seen in winter. The Elliptical Gall and Ball Gall are both found on the stem and are made by moths and flies. The third, known as the Bunch Gall, is formed at the tip of the stalk and appears as an intricate woody flower. (See Chapter 4.)

In snow around the stalks you may find tracks of Sparrows, Finches, or Juncos that have been feeding on the seeds. The uneaten seeds are scattered by the wind, giving rise to patches of Goldenrod even in abandoned lots of the

Shapes of Goldenrod stalks

city. Goldenrod is a perennial and, once rooted, will continue to grow in the same area. It does not do well in cultivated land, and its presence is a sign that the ground has lain fallow for at least a year.

Star-shaped flower parts of Goldenrod

In late winter, when the small seeds and delicate star-shaped flower parts are worn away by the wind, Goldenrod appears dried and lifeless, but in fact, many of the winter stalks are holding deep within their galls the developing life of next year's insects.

Heal-All (*Prunella vulgaris*)

Heal-All is a member of the Mint family but lacks any mint scent or flavor in winter. Its unusual flowerhead is

Heal-All

composed of tiers of hairy bracts topping a single stem. Two dried spines protrude from each tier. The small black seeds are probably shaken free by the wind and passing animals.

Heal-All flowerheads

The plant is a perennial and spreads by underground rootstocks, which periodically send up new stems; tolerant of a variety of conditions, growing in both shady and sunny areas. It does not form large stands or colonies, but is more commonly found as an isolated group along roadsides or in lawns.

Joe-Pye Weed (*Eupatorium* species)

Joe Pye, an American Indian living in colonial Massachusetts, had a native weed which he used to help cure European settlers of various illnesses. The plant became known by his name, but sole recognition was not really deserved,

Joe-Pye Weed

for Joe Pye's people as well as many other Indian tribes had known and used the plant long before.

The weed is tall, usually growing near open water or marshy areas, and during late summer and fall it puts forth a cluster of showy purple flowers. It is a member of the Composite family, as can be seen by the similarity of its flowers to those of Goldenrod and Aster. The plant is a native of North America and in its genus, *Eupatorium,* has many close relatives, including the Thoroughworts, Boneset, and Snakeroot.

Joe-Pye Weed flowerheads

The last of these, Snakeroot, is poisonous and was the cause of what early settlers called "milk sickness." When

Snakeroot was eaten by cows, the poison was passed on in their milk, often causing the death of whole families. But this genus need not leave a bad taste in your mouth, for remember that it also includes Joe-Pye Weed, one plant that can do more to help than harm.

Loosestrife (*Lythrum salicaria*)

Loosestrife, so prominent in summer with its purple flowers massing the edges of lakes and swamps, is deflatingly inconspicuous in its winter habit. Few people ever guess the real identity of this dried weed. In winter, Loosestrife's slender branches reach out and bend up beside the thin main stem. They are punctuated at even intervals by surrounding sets of flowerheads.

The plant is a strange mixture of geometry and numbers. The main stem tends to be hexagonal, the side branches

Purple Loosestrife

Loosestrife branching

square. The branches usually grow in whorls of three on the single main stem. Flower clusters grow in two's, three flowers in each cluster. Even more relationships between the plant parts exist, too lengthy to describe but easy to discover.

Purple Loosestrife, a native of Europe, is now the most widespread of its genus in North America. Look for the winter weed near lakes and by swamps; its upturned branches surrounded at even intervals by flowerheads are its characteristic mark. The generic name means "blood from wounds" and may be a reference to the plant's purple flowers or its bright red leaves in fall. The specific name, *salicaria*, means "willowlike" and refers to the shape of Loosestrife's leaves. Like Willows, Loosestrife grows near water, fulfilling much the same function as Cattails — slowly filling in sections of marshy areas.

Milkweed (*Asclepias* species)

The most enticing plant among winter weeds must be Milkweed, for who can resist taking handfuls of its silken seeds and tossing them into the wind? But the way these seeds

Milkweed pods and seeds

disperse when not interfered with is a more ordered event than their casual appearance would suggest.

The process starts with the pod splitting open and exposing the seeds, which are arranged so that they are released only a few at a time. Next, a few seeds separate from the others while remaining attached to the top of the pod by their filaments. This is important, for if the seeds just fell, most of them would land at the base of the parent plant and have to compete with each other. Finally, the wind separates the seeds from the pod and carries them across open fields. If the parachute of hollow filaments becomes trapped by a thicket or among grasses, the seed will separate from it and fall to the ground.

Milkweed grows in open meadows and barren lots. Its widespreading shallow root system, extending to a diameter of fifteen feet, makes it good for areas susceptible to erosion. In summer the plant is a stalk three feet high with lush green leaves; its veins, when broken, release a white milky sap from which the plant gets its name. Although not eaten by many animals, Milkweed's spring shoots are among the tastiest wild vegetables to be found. They can be eaten cooked like asparagus, or raw if they are still young and tender.

Certainly the winter stalk and pods of Milkweed are an inspired sculpture, but unless you want a snowstorm of Milkweed parachutes throughout your house, be sure they are empty before bringing them inside.

Motherwort (*Leonurus cardiaca*)

Motherwort is one of the tallest members of the Mint family growing in North America. Its strange name simply means "mother's plant" and may have been given because of an old belief that the plant could aid discomforts connected with pregnancy.

The fruits of the winter weed are particularly spiky; seeing these and its four-sided stem, it is impossible to mistake this plant for any other.

Motherwort is a perennial, for it lasts through the winter as a living rootstock which will continue to send up new stems each year.

The Mint family contains over three thousand species, most of which have square stems and glands in their leaves that produce odoriferous oils. Many of our cooking herbs are in this family, which includes Marjoram, Thyme, and Sage and other plants such as Rosemary, Lavender, and the familiar houseplant Coleus.

Motherwort flowerheads

Motherwort, although not native to North America, is nonetheless widespread throughout the Northeast, growing in the sunny areas of roadsides and undisturbed fields where so many of the winter weeds are found.

Mullein (*Verbascum thapsus*)

Mullein is certainly a bizarre form in the winter landscape. Appearing either as a giant candelabrum or a lone staff

Mullein

stuck in the ground, it may grow to heights of seven feet or more. It seems to favor the poorest of soils, often growing even in unplanted gravel by the sides of highways.

Mullein tops are encrusted with cuplike flower remains for up to three feet of their length; below, long leafy ridges line the stems. If you give the weed a shake, hundreds of small black seeds will pepper the snow below. These dried plants were once used as torches in Europe; dipped in tal-

Mullein flowerhead

low, they burned long, each empty flowerhead holding the solidifying fat.

Rosettes of large woolly leaves that you may find in winter are the first-year stage of Mullein's biennial growth. Like velvet to the touch, they are described by the common name which comes from the Latin *mollis,* meaning "soft." These rosettes are a favorite winter home for many insects.

Remembering a plant's whereabouts in summer or winter enables you come back and enjoy it during another stage when it might otherwise be hard to identify. Knowing the winter rosette, you can return in summer to see the large stalk of yellow flowers, so lovely that it is grown in cultivated gardens of Europe. Then later in the fall you can return again and enjoy the strange form of the winter weed.

Mustard (*Brassica* species)

Mustard is an easy plant to identify in the snow-draped road edges and neglected fields, for its slim transluscent membranes point upward along each part of its stem, giving the plant an airy featherlike quality.

Seeds, appearing as small black discs, may still be at-

Translucent pods of Mustard

tached to some of these membranes. It is these seeds, dark-colored in Black Mustard and light in White Mustard, that go into the familiar spreads so prevalent at baseball games and Sunday picnics. Uusally ground-up Black Mustard seeds are sold as dry mustard, whereas the spread is made from seeds of both white and black varieties, to which there has been added a mixture of vinegar and spices.

The generic name for Mustard, *Brassica,* means cabbage or cauliflower and reflects the close relationship among the three plants. In fact, Rutabaga, Cabbage, Kale, Cauliflower, Brussels sprouts, Turnip, and Kohlrabi are all in the same genus as Mustard. This relationship is also reflected in the facts that spring leaves of Mustard make a good potherb, and that the flowerheads can be eaten in the same manner as broccoli.

Another genus of the Mustard family is *Barbarea,* or Winter Cress. In the fall, this plant grows a rosette of distinctive

Mustard winter rosette

green leaves, which can be gathered throughout winter for use as salad greens.

Peppergrass (*Lepidium* species)

Peppergrass is probably more common in the city than in the country, being a familiar inhabitant of that unused space between sidewalk and city street, where trashcans wait to be emptied and where cars pull up, people step out, and

Peppergrass

dogs pause. The plant, seeming to favor this hardpacked earth, sends its single taproot deep into the soil to gather what moisture it can.

When the seeds of Peppergrass are newly matured they are thrown from the plant by an expulsive reaction within the pod. Those that remain on the stalk are often dispersed like the seeds of Tumbleweed, for the winter stalk, being

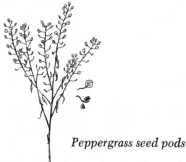

Peppergrass seed pods

brittle, lightweight, and generally spherical, may break off from its roots and be blown about by the wind, scattering seeds as it goes. This is particularly true of the city species *Lepidium virginicum*, which is short and stout, compared to its country cousin, Field Peppergrass (*Lepidium campestre*), which is too tall to tumble.

The spring shoots of Peppergrass are a good salad green, and the plant's common name refers to its pepperlike taste. Caution should be used, however, when gathering plants in the city, because of the likelihood that they have been polluted by the waste products of cars and dogs.

The generic name, *Lepidium*, comes from a word meaning "a small flake or scale" and describes the two ochre-colored seeds. City sparrows seem to enjoy these seeds, as is evidenced by the numerous bird tracks you will find in the snow beneath the plant. Besides having interesting habits, Peppergrass is always pleasant to see, for the transparent membranes dot its gracefully branching stalk, giving the whole plant the quality of intricate lace.

Ragweed (*Ambrosia* species)

Ragweed is known to most as the ubiquitous source of hayfever, but to birds it is a plentiful source of food. Its seeds,

Ragweed in winter

present after autumn, are one of the most valuable winter foods for all ground feeding birds. Among its admirers are the Sparrows, Finches, Juncos, Redpolls, and Bobwhites.

As most people know, Ragweed thrives in the city. The hundreds of seeds it produces may lie dormant up to five years, waiting for the slightest turn of the earth. Any gouge in the soil, or some loosened earth allows them to sprout into a ridiculously healthy crop of plants.

Having sprouted, the plant produces two types of flowers: greenish male flowers at the tips of the stems, and inconspicuous female flowers at the leaf axils. There are two

Ragweed's summer male flowers

main species: Common Ragweed (*Ambrosia artemisiifolia*), which grows to five feet tall on dry soil, and Great Ragweed (*Ambrosia trifida*), which, loving moister areas, grows to a towering fifteen feet. The seeds of Great Ragweed are less useful to wildlife because of their tough outer coating.

The common name, Ragweed, comes from the ragged appearance of the plant's deeply cut leaves. The generic name, *Ambrosia,* was given by the Roman natural historian Pliny and seems to be a misnomer. One of its meanings is "food for the gods," which should be changed to "food for the birds," or for those who get hayfever, to just "for the birds."

St. Johnswort (*Hypericum perforatum*)

An old country custom in Europe was to hang a special yellow-blossomed plant in your window on the eve of St. John's Day (June 24), in order to repel bad spirits and counteract the evil eye. In general, the presence of this plant was considered a good omen, and since it was thought that the plant warded off lightning and revealed the identity of passing witches, St. Johnswort was allowed to prosper around the farmhouse. It became known as St. John's Plant or St. Johnswort (*wort* meaning "plant" or "herb"). When

St. Johnswort flowerhead

the plant immigrated to North America it left its traditions behind, and although still as effective as it probably ever was against evil, St. Johnswort is now seldom used for that purpose.

The side branches of St. Johnswort grow in perfect pairs off the central stem. At the end of each branch there are numerous cupped seed containers, each of which holds over a hundred minute, shiny black seeds. As the plant is swayed by wind, the seeds fall out and are blown to areas nearby. It has no known wildlife use, but its red-brown stems are certainly a pleasant touch of color in the winter landscape.

Sensitive Fern (*Onoclea sensibilis*)

Sensitive Fern often baffles winter plant enthusiasts, for it differs so from other weeds. It has no remains of leaves, it is

Sensitive Fern spore cases

never in bloom, it lasts over two years, and its capsules, when broken, contain only "brown dust." Knowing that the plant is part of a fern helps some people but confuses others.

Ferns reproduce by spores rather than by seeds. The brown dust in the capsules is actually hundreds of thousands of spores, which will be dispersed by wind in dry weather. Fern spores, when they sprout, do not grow into a

Sensitive Fern summer fronds

plant of the same shape as the one they came from, but each grows into a small heart-shaped leaf no taller than ½ inch. This new tiny plant reproduces sexually, growing both egg and sperm cells. The fertilized egg then sprouts tall, green, leafy fronds — what we normally think of as ferns. Along with the green fronds it grows the spore-bearing stalk. The fronds die back after the first fall frost, but the spore-bearing stalk remains standing through the winter and into the next summer.

Sensitive Fern is one of the few ferns with such a hardy spore-bearing stalk, and it is frequently found growing near wet areas. In late winter you may find the spore cases already broken open and emptied by the action of early spring moisture and warmth.

Spiraea (*Spiraea* species)

Spiraea is one of the few winter weeds whose stalks remain alive in winter. Since it is a deciduous plant, it is often

Spiraea flowerheads

considered a shrub. It drops its leaves in fall, revealing a smooth reddish brown stem, which in spring puts forth new leaves. At the top of the winter stalk are jewellike minute flowerheads. Their five-part structure hints at the plant's membership in the Rose family, and their tiny beauty should not be missed.

Meadowsweet and Steeplebush

Steeplebush and Meadowsweet are the two species of *Spiraea* most commonly found. They are easily told apart even in winter, for the flowers of Steeplebush are arranged into a slender pointed steeple, while those of Meadowsweet form a broad rounded top. Both typically grow in little

Meadowsweet with Sparrow's nest

groves among the grasses of old open meadows. There are often sparrows' nests and occasionally hornets' nests built among them, because of the cover they afford in summer.

The generic name, *Spiraea*, means "herbs for garlands." It was probably given to the plants because their strong flexible stems lined with leaves and topped with showy flowers made them ideal for weaving into garlands and summer wreaths. Meadowsweet and Steeplebush are natives of North America and grow most commonly on rocky soil of northeastern coastal states and Southern Canada.

Teasel (*Dipsacus* species)

Teasel forms an exciting design among the winter weeds. Covered with stiff thorns, it is hostile to the touch but fascinating to the eye. Look for the marvelous geometric arrangement of spines on the dried flowerheads. Woody

Teasel flowerhead

bracts encircling the flowerheads often bend into perfect curlicues at their tips. Also notice how thorns grow out of long ridges that line the branches and stem.

Teasel is a native of Europe and Asia and has long been used in wool processing. The dried flowerheads, split and placed on rollers, were used to card, or tease, wool, giving

Teasel

some of the common names for the plant: Teasel and Fuller's Teasel.

The plant is a biennial, growing a hardy rosette the first year and a zesty stalk the second. The plant, rare on the East Coast, is common from central New York to the Midwest. If you wear heavy gloves when picking it and have a floor vase to put the tall stalk in, Teasel's intricate designs can be a great source of visual enjoyment throughout the winter.

Tansy (*Tanacetum vulgare*)

Tansy's rosette of leaves that lasts into winter is a real odoriferous treat. Dig down through the snow at the base of the winter stalk to get a small piece of one of the green fernlike leaves, crush it between your fingers, and smell it. The rich odor comes from an oil in the leaves that has been used for such varied purposes as baking, easing sunburn pain, and repelling insects. In large doses the oil is poisonous.

The winter stalk of Tansy has a group of small brown "buttons" at its top, arranged in a flat cluster. Take one of these buttons and rub its surface; the seeds will break off in

Tansy

your hand. They are thin and packed into a hemisphere on the flowerhead. From July to September these buttons are bright yellow, and if picked and crushed together, can be the start of a good yellow dye.

Tansy, a native of Europe, has been grown in European gardens for centuries, and herbalists have ascribed many cures to its use. Today we no longer use it — in fact few

Tansy winter rosette

Tansy flowerheads

people even notice it — though it fills city lots and lines country roads with fragrant leaves and button-topped stalks.

Thistle (*Circium* species)

Whatever you do, don't try to gather Thistles, for there is no way to come close to them without getting stabbed by sharp thorns. The stems, leaves, and even flowers are thorned. The thorns keep us as well as some grazing animals away from

Thistle

the plant. Just look across any well-grazed meadow and you will spot the Thistles, untouched and surrounded by close-cropped grass. Their protection allows the plant to mature unharmed, and leaves it basking in the sun without a leafy competitor in sight.

You might think this would be enough to insure the sur-

Thistle flowerhead

vival of any self-respecting plant, but the Thistle takes it even farther. First, it produces an average of 4,000 seeds per plant — seeds that are protected, while developing, by a spined container and that have their own parachute of filaments when they are released. The filaments are similar to Milkweed's except that each filament is lined with further small hairs, increasing wind resistance tremendously. A Thistle seed in still air will take 10 seconds to float just 6 feet to the ground.

Besides the seeds and thorns, Thistles have evolved a long taproot that grows 6 feet down. It cannot be pulled up, and if the upper plant is cut off there is enough stored food in the root to send up new shoots. In one common species, Canada Thistle (*Circium arvense*), lateral rootstocks grow off the main taproot. At intervals along these rootstocks there are nodes, which in turn send up new shoots above the ground. This is vegetative reproduction: one plant producing another without the seed state intervening. These rootstocks can grow as long as 20 feet in one season. If a cultivator runs over a rootstock and chops it up, each piece can then develop into a new plant.

No protection in nature is perfect, however, for some other organism will always evolve a way either to overcome it or to use it to its own advantage, like the Goldfinch, which eats the Thistle seeds and makes its nest with the filaments, or the beetle, which lays its eggs inside the flower, where its hatched larvae will be both safe and well-fed.

Thistle thorns

Vervain (*Verbena* species)

Vervain's branches, all reaching toward the sky, are slender, and seed-coated at their tips, making the plant appear more delicate than most of its winter companions. Its appearance has led it to be used as an ornamental flower in cultivated gardens.

Blue Vervain and White Vervain

Two species of Vervain are common, and, unlike most other winter weeds, these two can be easily distinguished in their dried form. White Vervain (*Verbena urticifolia*) has seeds intermittently spaced along its branch tips, whereas the branches of Blue Vervain (*Verbena hastata*) are solidly

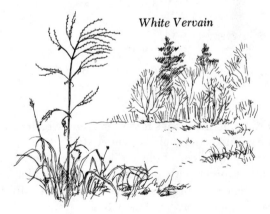

White Vervain

coated with seeds. Both species grow up to 5 feet tall in sun-filled habitats.

Vervain has a square stem but is not part of the Mint family, which also has square stems. Its numerous seeds are eaten only occasionally by birds, but the California Indians were known to gather, roast, and grind them for use in making breadstuffs. Vervain is a perennial and a native of North America. It rarely grows in colonies, more commonly being found as isolated plants in roadsides and waste spaces.

Wild Carrot (*Daucus carota*)

Wild Carrot, better known to some as Queen Anne's Lace, is a close relative of our domestic carrot. This becomes clear

Wild Carrot

when you examine the plant's first-year stage, which can be seen usually near the base of the winter stalk. Its rosette of leaves is exactly like a carrot top and if pulled up will reveal a thick white taproot with both the shape and odor of a small carrot. Since the plant is a biennial, it is not until the second year that it produces a stalk with flowers.

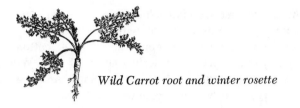

Wild Carrot root and winter rosette

The intricate lace quality of these flowers has earned the plant its other name, Queen Anne's Lace. The shape of the flowerhead is called umbellate, which means "shaped like an umbrella"; this is the characteristic flower shape of all plants in the order Umbellales. In summer the flower opens and closes in relation to the humidity of the surrounding air, and a similar mechanism may again be used in the fall, when the flower bracts close around the matured seeds, holding them in what is commonly described as a "bird's nest."

The seeds, small and lined with four rows of spines, are dispersed by animals, whose fur picks up the seeds as they pass by. Wild Carrot seeds can be gathered and steeped in hot water to make a good-tasting tea — fun to make after a winter walk. If you bite one of the seeds in the field you will find its flavor similar to that of cooked carrots. The seeds can be used as a spice; in fact, many plants from which we get spices are related to Wild Carrot, such as Caraway, Fennel, Coriander, Anise, and Parsley.

Wild Carrot flowerheads

After the first snowfall Wild Carrot's flowerheads again become white, this time not with lace but with puffs of fresh snow, giving the appearance of a cotton plant strangely out of place. Formerly a native of Asia, Wild Carrot is now thoroughly naturalized in North America, thriving in city lots as well as in country meadows.

Yarrow (*Achillea millefolium*)

A Yarrow stalk broken off near the top makes a perfect miniature tree or shrub for the landscapes of train sets and model buildings. Its flat-topped cluster of flowers is a good example of nature grouping a number of small flowers into one showy bunch, more attractive to insects.

Yarrow flowerheads

Yarrow winter rosette

In some ways Yarrow's winter stalk is like a small version of Tansy; like Tansy, it has fragrant leaves. Brush the snow away from the base and crush one of the leaves that form a rosette around the stalk. They smell strong and spicy. Some people use them to make a tea that induces sweating.

The leaves are finely cut like a ragged feather, and Yarrow's specific name describes this: *millefolium*, or thousand-leaved. Its generic name, *Achillea,* refers to its association

Yarrow

with Achilles, who, as the legend goes, used the leaves to stop the bleeding from the wounds of his soldiers. Some herbalists go even further, claiming it will cure baldness and purge the soul (but not claiming any connection between the two).

Yarrow's success in populating the land is due in part to its growth patterns. Being a perennial, it comes up each year from the same widespreading set of roots, sometimes producing flowers in both spring and fall. In addition, each flowering produces thousands of seeds, which are small, light, and easily carried on the wind. It is no wonder that it is as common in the city as in the country.

II

Snow

*E*ACH YEAR SNOW RENEWS our sense of wonder. The first flakes are always magical, their slow whitening of the landscape drawing us irresistibly out of doors. Do other animals see snow as we do? They may wonder at snow, but above all, their instincts prepare them to deal with it as a

Seeds being dispersed over the snow's hard crust

physical force in their lives, a force that can freeze or warm, feed or starve, trap or free. We have to deal with snow for only as long as it takes us to shovel our walks and plow our streets, but animals have to cope with it constantly. Many animals must travel on a razor's edge between survival and death; snow, by its character or depth, can easily throw them to one side or the other.

Every form of life is affected differently by the depth of snow. Even as little as an inch hides the daily movements of Meadow Mice from the keen eyes of their predators; this same depth also hinders Bobwhites as they feed, because it covers seeds and insects from their view. Slightly deeper snow forms an insulating layer over the land, keeping dormant insects, plants, and small mammals protected from drying and chilling winds, yet allowing the sun's radiant energy to penetrate.

As the snow becomes deeper, it creates more problems for

Under a young Spruce in deep snow is a shelter for Grouse or Rabbits.

animals. A Red Fox can walk easily in six inches of snow, but when the snow is deeper, the animal must bound through it, expending more energy and catching its prey less often. A hunger-weakened White-tailed Deer can actually be immobilized by deep drifts, and even healthy deer will have more difficulty escaping a Bobcat attack. But for the Cottontail Rabbit, deep snow provides food; since it feeds on the winter buds of sapling trees, the deeper snow helps it to reach more buds.

The character of snow is as important as its depth. Snow can be fluffy, wind-packed, wet, thinly crusted, glazed, or dry and drifting. These qualities hurt or help each plant and animal in a different way, and the adaptations and instincts of different species determine whether or not they can use the qualities of snow to their own advantage.

The presence of snow over thousands of years has favored certain physical adaptations of plants and animals. Birches are small trees with fine branches; the weight of the snow and ice bends them to the ground, but their trunks are flexible even in winter, and the trees spring back up when the snow melts. The Long-tailed Weasel turns white in winter so that it is hidden from both predators and prey. The Ruffed Grouse grows combs on the sides of its toes to support it better on the snow. The Lynx and Snowshoe Hare, also, have large feet which support them on the surface, enabling them to live farther north than other cats and hares.

Snow bending Birches

Snow shapes the behavior of animals as well. Wolves travel on the wind-packed snow of northern lakes. Otters combine sliding and bounding to travel overland in late winter. Deer stay in the shallow snow under spruces, taking

Spruce needles catching snow

advantage of the fact that a third of the snow accumulation is held in the branches above. Bobcats travel on the trails of humans and other animals to avoid the uncertainty of unaltered snow. And Ruffed Grouse dive into powdery snow to keep warm at night.

These are just a few examples of the hundreds of ways in which plants and animals specifically interact with snow.

Shallow snow under a fallen log forms a runway for Squirrels and rodents.

But snow affects nature on an even larger scale. By protecting insects from ground feeding birds, small mammals from predators, and green plants from browsers, it increases their populations and the diversity of their types in both winter and summer. And, on the other hand, by limiting the food of birds, predators, and browsers, it limits the populations and diversity of these animals. So, in a very direct way, snow controls the character and composition of life throughout the year, and learning its ways as well as how life is affected by it is essential to understanding the ecology of the north.

To some extent, the snow cover itself is influenced by the types of snow crystals within it. This influence is usually greatest at the time of a storm, for snow crystals, once fallen, tend to change into similarly shaped ice granules. But as the snow falls the crystal type will determine how much the snow adheres, packs, builds up, or drifts.

Snow crystals form in clouds where temperatures are anywhere from 32° to −39°F. These clouds are made up of water droplets so microscopic that thousands could fit on the dot of an *i*. We see them as a cloud only because such vast numbers are concentrated in one area. Along with the droplets there are minute particles of dust and salt from the surface of the earth and sea that have been carried miles up into the sky by prevailing winds.

These cooled particles have the physical property of attracting water molecules from the microscopic droplets in the cloud. As these molecules gather on the particle, they freeze and build ice crystals. This is the start of a snowflake or snow crystal.

As these crystals become larger they begin to fall, often hitting other crystals. The result is that part of the crystal breaks off and becomes the center or "nucleus" for another crystal. This occurrence often causes a chain reaction that in turn starts other crystals growing, and is believed to result in the sudden bursts of heavy snowfall we often experience during a snowstorm.

Which one of seven common shapes a crystal will be is determined by the temperature and humidity of the air in which the crystal is formed. If the air is cold and there is little moisture, then the very small column crystals are formed. If the air is warmer and there is lots of moisture, then the stellar crystals have a better chance of forming. Since it is also common for a crystal to pass through a number of atmospheric conditions before it lands, it may start off as a hexagonal plate, go through the conditions of stellar formation, and then go back through the conditions that will form a plate.

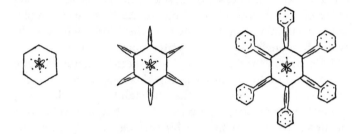

Another crystal might start out as a column crystal and then pass through the conditions that produce plate crystals. Often snow crystals that are formed at warmer temperatures will collide and stick together. Then they fall as large

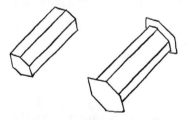

conglomerate flakes that may be as big as 2 inches in diameter. Conglomerate flakes also form when the crystal structure is intricate enough to interlock with other crystals.

Once snow crystals land on the ground, they start to lose their fine detail through a process called metamorphosis or sublimation. In sublimation the fine outer parts of the crystal evaporate and condense on the larger central part of the crystal. In this way, almost all fallen crystals soon change into small granules of ice.

SNOW, RAIN, SLEET, AND HAIL

Snow starts as a nucleus of dust or salt that attracts molecules of water from cloud droplets. As these water molecules accumulate on the nucleus, they form ice crystals, which become larger as more water molecules are added.

Rain starts as the microscopic droplets in clouds that are so concentrated that they join together into larger droplets. They soon become so heavy that they fall to the earth.

Sleet starts as rain, then passes through a very cold layer of air on its way to the earth's surface. At this point the droplets freeze into solid icy raindrops and continue falling.

Hail starts as sleet but is thrown back into the raincloud by thunderstorm updrafts. In the raincloud the droplets pick up another coating of water and fall again. This process continues until the strong updrafts can no longer keep the drops in the air. Hailstones, which can be up to 3 inches in diameter, are the largest precipitate that falls from the sky.

Key to Snow Crystals

Snow-crystal-watching opens up a world of discovery each time it snows. The crystals are not only a never-ending type of aesthetic enjoyment, but they also indicate the type of snow cover that will result — whether it will be good for tracking, will break limbs off trees, will form huge drifts, and so on. The crystals are usually variations on a small number of basic shapes. There are illustrations below of the shapes and their combinations, followed by more detailed descriptions of the characteristics of the crystals and the types of clouds they form in. By checking the snowflakes in a storm more than once you can see the progression of crystal types, for they usually change in the course of a given snowfall.

Crystal-watching is best done by catching snowflakes on a dark surface such as the arm of your jacket or sweater. Some of the crystals will be too tiny to appreciate without a small magnifying glass, but most are easy to enjoy with the unaided eye. As you bend close to see them, try to avoid melting them with your breath.

SIMPLE CRYSTALS

MAGNIFIED	LARGEST ACTUAL SIZE TO BE SEEN	NAME
		*Hexagonal Plate Crystal*

MAGNIFIED	*LARGEST ACTUAL SIZE TO BE SEEN*	*NAME*
		*Stellar Crystal, or Dendrite*

		Column Crystal
		Needle Crystal

MAGNIFIED	LARGEST ACTUAL SIZE TO BE SEEN	NAME

Asymmetrical Crystal

Graupel

Powder Snow

COMBINATION CRYSTALS

These are crystals that are composed of more than one basic type.

MAGNIFIED	LARGEST ACTUAL SIZE TO BE SEEN	NAME

Tsuzumi Crystal

	LARGEST	
MAGNIFIED	*ACTUAL SIZE*	*NAME*
	TO BE SEEN	

Bullet Crystal

Spatial Dendrite

*Hexagonal Plates
with Stellar
Formations*

*Stellar Crystals with
Hexagonal Plate
Formations*

Natural History Descriptions

SIMPLE CRYSTALS

HEXAGONAL PLATE CRYSTAL   This is a six-sided, flat crystal with varying degrees of design on its surface. The largest size to be seen is ³⁄₁₆ inch in diameter, but about half that size is more common. They are always only a small per-

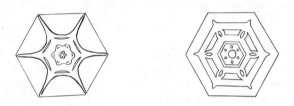

centage of all the snowflakes in a storm and often appear along with Stellar Crystals. Since they have no projections, they do not interlock, but drift freely.

I find these a particular joy to come across, because they represent a perfect hexagon in nature and they reflect light off their surfaces.

STELLAR CRYSTAL OR DENDRITE   As the name indicates, this type is shaped like a star with six points radiating from the center. The points can be any shape, from a simple spike to an elaborate design. These crystals are what we typically

think of as snowflakes. The largest size to be seen is ½ inch in diameter. Stellar crystals form only a small percentage of any storm; they often occur with Hexagonal Plate Crystals.

Stellar Crystals form in low clouds where the temperature is not too cold and where there is plenty of moisture. Because of their intricate design, they often interlock while falling, ending as large conglomerate flakes, sometimes as much as 2 inches in diameter, that drift slowly to the ground. The flakes, since they will readily hold together, stack on the tops of branches and street signs. Because of their slow falling, Stellar Crystals create a peaceful effect during a snowfall.

COLUMN CRYSTAL   Column Crystals are small six-sided columns with flat or pointed ends. The largest size likely to be seen is ¼ inch in length. These crystals often have hollow air spaces inside them, but this is hard to observe because the crystals are so small. They are not a common crystal.

They form in very cold clouds where there is little moisture. Extremely high clouds that appear like pulled wisps of cotton, called cirrus clouds or mares' tails, are made almost entirely of these crystals in winter. When clouds with these crystals pass in front of the moon, they create a beautiful colored halo around it.

NEEDLE CRYSTAL   This is a long, slender, six-sided column with fine points projecting from either end. Extremely common crystals, they can account for much of a storm's accumulation. They range in length from ¼ to ⅜ inch and

often freeze together, forming conglomerate flakes. These conglomerate flakes fall slowly to the ground but seem to break into many splinters of ice when they land on a hard surface.

ASYMMETRICAL CRYSTAL   These groups of platelike crystals, joined together in an irregular shape, are another

common type to fall in our snows. When they join to form conglomerate flakes, they can be mistaken at a distance for Stellar Crystals. The largest size to be seen is approximately ⅜ inch in diameter.

GRAUPEL   Graupel are small pellets of snow, actually small Hexagonal Plate or Stellar Crystals that became coated with frozen droplets (rime) as they fell through moisture-laden clouds. The shape of the original crystal is usually obscured or only partially visible. Graupel tend to fall in short concentrated showers within a longer snowstorm. When they hit the ground, they bounce off hard objects.

POWDER CRYSTALS   This snow gets its name from its minute granular quality. It is known best by skiers, for since it does not pack, it makes good skiing. Although the crystals seem like small grains of snow, they are really minute col-

umns and plates connected to each other in irregular formations too small to be distinguished by the naked eye.

COMBINATION CRYSTALS

The following are crystals that have started in one atmospheric condition and traveled through one or more different conditions before they land.

TSUZUMI CRYSTAL   This is a Column Crystal with a Hexagonal Plate Crystal at either end; it is named after a type of Japanese drum that has a similar appearance.

STELLAR HEXAGONAL PLATE CRYSTALS   These are either Hexagonal Plate Crystals that went through Stellar Crystal cloud conditions, or Stellar Crystals that went through Hex-

agonal Plate cloud conditions. They are quite common and form some of the most spectacular crystal shapes.

BULLET CRYSTALS   These are Column Crystals with hexa-

gonal pyramids at one end, joined together with others of the same type.

SPATIAL DENDRITE   Spatial Dendrites are feathery Stellar Crystals with other points projecting at 90° angles from each of the six original points.

III

Wintering Trees

TREES ARE PLANTS that have evolved woody stems so that their leaves will be supported in the air, thus avoiding the competition for sunlight at ground level. As with all green plants, their first priority must be to place their leaves in sunlight, for the sun is the primal source of their energy. This striving to arrange leaves in light is most clearly shown in the winter trees. Here in the outlines of their bare branches hundreds of solutions are revealed, each species a distinct linear sculpture created jointly by the forces of light and life.

Two basic forms are immediately evident in the branching of trees. One is a single main trunk with branches radiating off it; the other, a trunk that splits above the ground into many smaller trunks. The first form is conical and pointed, like Cedars, Pines, and Spruces, the second spreading and rounded, like Oaks, Elms, and Sycamores.

Not all branches on a tree grow at the same rate. Some trees have two types of branches: long shoots, which grow quickly, forming large, long branches that create the basic pattern of the tree, and short shoots, which grow slowly, forming the smaller twigs that fill in the spaces between the branches and generally hold the leaves. The ratio of long shoots to short shoots and their placement determines much of the overall character of the tree; they make it seem full or open, heavy or delicate.

But the growth pattern of a tree and its particular arrangement of leaves in light is very elastic. It can be stretched, shrunk, pulled, or twisted, depending on its environment and the competition for sunlight. Trees in open fields may display their purest shapes in relation to light, but even there, a constant wind can stunt them. Forest trees are stretched tall, clear of branches until near the top, with a small flattened crown that carves a territory out of the forest canopy. Those at the edges of meadows, lakes, or rivers grow into the open space, leaning away from their competitors.

Besides this display of form, what is a tree doing in winter? How will it know when to put forth leaves in spring? Why did it drop them in the fall?

To plants, winter is a time of drought. Most water is frozen within the ground or above it as snow, and is therefore unavailable to them. Winter's drought lasts six months or more and is a serious condition to which plants must adapt.

Since the summer processes of food production and growth use tremendous amounts of water, they must stop in winter. These processes are centered in the leaf; therefore trees in temperate climates drop their leaves in fall and seal over the point of attachment with a corky layer. Even next year's leaves, neatly miniaturized in the winter buds, are covered over with moisture-conserving scales. Trees that keep their leaves, notably the evergreens, have adaptations which conserve water — thin or small needlelike leaves with waxy coatings.

But a tree doesn't just grow in summer and stop in winter; it continually alternates the parts of it that grow, channeling energy to some, withholding it from others.

For example, trees in summer have already grown their next year's leaves, neatly miniaturized and contained within scale-covered buds. In late summer the tree keeps these leaves from expanding and growing, while at the same time, maturing the present year's seeds and fruits.

Trees in winter must also control their growth. They must carefully time the opening of leaves and flowers in spring to avoid injury by heavy frost. To do this, they cannot rely solely on temperature or availability of water, for they might be "fooled" by late winter thaws. They must respond to more consistent measures, such as the timed break-down of chemicals within their cells, or the changing ratios of light to dark that reflect the solar season.

So the image of the wintering tree as a symbol of death and emptiness must itself die, for in reality, winter trees already contain the coming year's leaves and flowers, continually respond to light and temperature in the environment, and in their silhouettes, graphically represent the reaching out of life to absorb energy from the sun.

Key to Wintering Trees

Trees are really not hard to identify in winter, especially if you concentrate on the most common ones first. When you have learned to recognize the six most common deciduous trees and the evergreen trees, you will know at least 80 percent of the trees found in most northern forests.

The first section lists the six most common deciduous trees and gives short descriptions and illustrations that will enable you to identify them. This is where to start; continue to find and identify these six and your ability to make distinctions between winter trees will keep improving.

When you know these trees well, pick a new tree that you often come across. Look at its buds, bark, and branching, and any other feature such as seeds or dead leaves. Then go to the list of remaining trees and find one whose important characteristics are the same as those of your tree. If for some reason you can't find it, don't despair; just remember the tree and try another.

When a leaf falls from a tree, a small mark, called the leaf scar, remains where the leaf was attached. Just above the recent leaf scars are small buds, which contain next year's leaves and flowers. These buds, called leaf buds or flower buds, are different for each tree, and are often used for identification in winter.

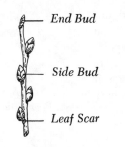

End Bud

Side Bud

Leaf Scar

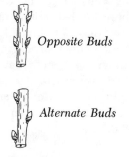

Opposite Buds

Alternate Buds

THE SIX MOST COMMON TREES

OAK — Oak has clusters of four or more buds at the ends of its twigs. These buds usually vary in size. Oaks, especially younger trees, may also have brown, leathery leaves still attached to their branches all through winter.

MAPLE AND ASH — There are only four native trees in our northern woods with opposite branching — Dogwood, Buckeye, Maple, and Ash — and by far the most common are Maple and Ash. These two can be told apart by their distinctive end buds. Ash's end bud is dark and dome-shaped.

Ash
End Bud

Maple buds are oval and between ¼ inch and ½ inch in length. No other opposite branching tree has buds that look like them except Buckeyes. Since Buckeye end buds are well over ½ inch long, it's easy to tell Buckeye and Maple buds apart.

Maple Twigs and End Buds

BEECH — You can identify Beech by its buds or its bark. The buds are brown to beige, long, and pointed, unlike those of any other tree. Beech bark is light silver-gray, and smooth. Other trees may have smooth gray bark when young, but with age it splits and fissures, whereas Beech bark remains smooth even when the tree is old.

Beech Buds

BIRCH — There are two ways to identify all Birches. One is by the long, thin horizontal lines that mark the bark; the other is by the catkins that hang from the tips of the upper branches. Some other trees have one or the other of these characteristics, but only Birches have both. The bark of some Birch trees is very white, that of others is silvery; still others have black bark.

Horizontal Lines on Birch Bark

ASPEN — Two things will help you identify Aspens in winter. First, they grow as a group of small trees in a waste area or forest edge. Second, the smooth, light bark of their upper trunks has a greenish tinge. Where they grow is as important as what they look like, for Aspens typically like

Birch   Catkins

open sunny waste spaces such as old fields, the land along turnpikes, or old gravel pits and dumps. Here they quickly form small groups of short-lived trees, usually under 25 feet tall. Their light-colored, smooth bark with its greenish tinge, once recognized, is the most striking feature to help you identify them.

Aspen buds are variable in size, color and texture but always sharply pointed. Quaking Aspen has dark, shiny brown buds (see illustration), while Bigtooth Aspen has grayish downy buds.

Quaking Aspen Twig and Buds

TREES WITH NEEDLES OR CONES

PINE — Long, thin needles attached in bundles of 5, 3, or 2.

CEDAR — Small, scalelike needles arranged along twigs.

Pine Needles

Cedar Needles

HEMLOCK — Flat needles with two white lines on the underside. Short stem between needle and twig. Needles ± ½ inch long.

Hemlock Needles

BALSAM FIR — Flat needles, slightly rounded at ends, with two white lines on the underside. No stem on needle. Needles ± 1 inch long.

SPRUCE — Generally, four-sided (not flat) needles. Needle sharply pointed.

LARCH — No needles on tree in winter, but small cones usually present. Stubby twigs on branches.

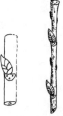

Larch Cone and Branch

The rest of the deciduous trees are listed in order, starting with the most common. Each of these trees has two characteristics listed next to it. To identify a tree, simply read the first characteristic listed next to each name until you find one that describes your tree. If the first feature given matches your tree, read the second also. If both match, then you have identified the tree. If a second characteristic is in parentheses, it means that the first clue is enough for positive identification.

TREES WITHOUT GREEN NEEDLES OR CONES

ELM — Side buds placed off-center from leaf scar. (Trunk often divides into many other, smaller trunks.)

Elm Buds

Branching of American Elm

WILLOW — Single scale covers leaf buds. (Twigs colored yellow or orange.)

Willow Buds

CHERRY — Thick horizontal markings on dark bark of upper trunk and branches. Bark of young twigs tastes like stale cigars. (Just take a small taste.)

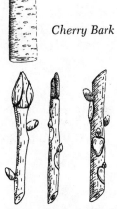

Cherry Bark

HICKORY — Large alternate leaf scars. End buds large and ovate (egg-shaped), or thinner and mustard yellow in color.

Hickory   Hickory
End Buds   Leaf Scars

LOCUST — Thorns: small and paired on twigs, or long and branched on trunk. (Flattened bean pods on tree or on ground beneath.)

Honey Locust Bean Pod

Black Locust Bean Pods

BASSWOOD — Buds waxy red with only two scales covering each bud. (Seeds possibly still on tree.)

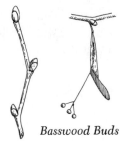

Basswood Buds

Basswood Seeds

SYCAMORE — Irregular patches of whitish bark under peeling, darker, outer bark. Seed balls handing off twig ends.

Sycamore Seed Cluster

POPLAR — Long, pointed end buds: sticky, or fragrant when rubbed. Alternate side buds diverge from twig.

Poplar Buds

TULIP TREE — Beige seeds arranged in flowerlike clusters on upper twigs. End buds dark green and flattened like a duck's bill.

Tulip Tree Seed Cluster

BUCKEYE — Opposite side buds. Large ovate end buds, more than ½ inch long.

Buckeye Buds

SASSAFRAS — Dark green twigs and end buds. Twigs have lemony odor when scratched or lemon taste when chewed.

Sassafras Twig

DOGWOOD — Opposite side buds and leaf scars. End buds shaped in either of two ways.

Dogwood End Buds

APPLE — Many 1-inch-long twigs that look like thorns. These short twigs have raised leaf scars or many lines encircling them.

Crabapple Twig   *Apple Twig*

HAWTHORN — Long, smooth, un-branched thorns. (Small, densely branched tree.)

Hawthorn Thorns

HOP HORNBEAM — Small catkins on upper branches, in groups of three. Bark has many thin, vertical, flaking strips.

Hop Hornbeam Catkins

HORNBEAM — Smooth, sinewy, dark gray bark on small tree; often more than one trunk together. Thin, polished, dark red twigs.

WALNUT — Large, alternate leaf scars. Furry moustache above leaf scar; or side buds downy, gray, and globular.

Walnut Side Buds

Walnut Leaf Scars

SHRUBS

Although shrubs are too numerous to cover adequately in this guide, I have included Blueberry, Sumac, Alder, and Hobblebush because they are common in the North, and Witch Hazel because its fruit capsules are so outstanding.

High Bush Blueberry
Vaccinium corymbosum

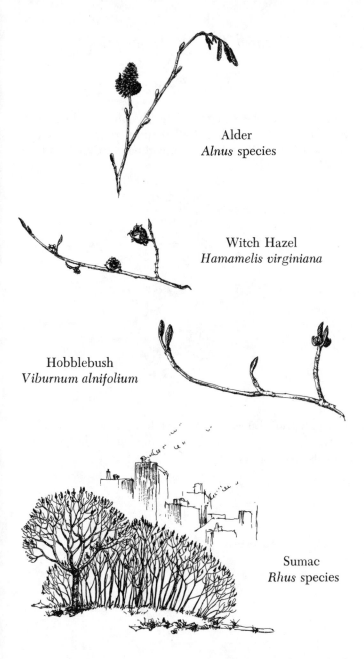

Alder
Alnus species

Witch Hazel
Hamamelis virginiana

Hobblebush
Viburnum alnifolium

Sumac
Rhus species

Natural History Descriptions

Apple (*Malus* species)

Apple trees can be recognized by the short stubby twigs which line their branches. Called spurs, they grow only a fraction of an inch each year, providing sturdy support for

Apple

the heavy fruit. Lines closely encircle them, each one representing a year's growth. Cherry trees and other orchard trees also have spurs.

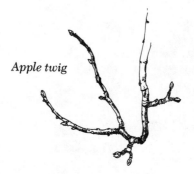

Apple twig

Our only native apple trees are the Crabapples. The trees that produce our market apples were brought from Europe by early settlers. Strangely enough, commercial Apple trees do not grow true from seed. In other words, if you plant a seed from a McIntosh apple, it will produce fruit slightly different from the McIntosh; they may be more tasty or, more likely, less so. Therefore, there are hundreds of varieties of Apples and Crabapples, only a few of which have worked their way into the stomachs of avid apple eaters. Many of these varieties have been discovered by chance, like the McIntosh Apple, which was discovered by John McIntosh in Ontario as he was clearing his forest. Other varieties have been produced through careful hybridization. When a good variety is found it must be continued by cuttings and graftings rather than by seeds.

Both wild and cultivated apples are enjoyed by wildlife.

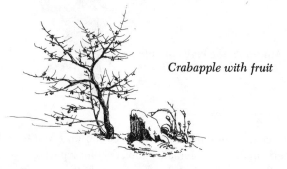

Crabapple with fruit

When the fruit is ripe, Foxes, Deer, Raccoons, and birds come out of the woods to eat them. Insect larvae also feed on apples, and Yellow Jackets especially enjoy the rotting fruit.

Native Crabapples are small trees with fruit varying in quality almost always too sour to eat right off the tree, but always delicious when made into jellies. Sometimes their fruit hangs on the trees through the winter, and a Crabapple tree can startle the observer with its apparent abundance in the midst of the surrounding winter scarcity.

Ash (*Fraxinus* species)

Ash trees, somewhat undistinguished-looking but extremely hardy, are one of the four common trees with opposite leaf buds and opposite branching. Their leaf scars are easily seen near the branch tips. Ashes grow well in average soils and usually grow scattered throughout a forest, rarely forming stands of more than a few trees.

Four species grow in the area covered by this guide, all very similar in appearance and each with a color name:

Ash trunk, showing opposite branching of twigs

White, Green, Blue, and Black Ash. Green and White Ash bear their male and female flowers on separate trees, whereas Blue and Black Ash often have both sexes on the same tree. The seeds, bearing attached wings, mature in the fall. They hang in clusters on the branches well into winter,

Ash seeds

and when falling twirl in the air like a one-bladed propeller. The wing slows the fall and allows more time for wind to disperse the seeds away from the parent plant.

Although abundant, Ashes have never been of more than

Ash twig and buds

moderate value to wildlife. However, Finches, Grosbeaks, and Cardinals do eat the seeds in fall and early winter; Beaver and Porcupine occasionally eat the bark, and Deer and Rabbits will chew a sapling's twigs down to mere nubs.

Where Ash comes closest to distinction is in the quality of its wood. Almost all wood sports equipment is Ash. Baseball bats, hockey sticks, tennis rackets, oars, snowshoes, skis, bowling alleys, and the handles of garden tools are all made of Ash. This is because Ash is light and strong, can take stress, and is just pliant enough to have some spring and resilience. Other woods, such as Oak and Hickory, may be stronger, but they are also heavier. Some of you may have Black Ash picnic baskets that belonged to your parents or grandparents. The American Indians taught the settlers how to pound Black Ash until it split along its growth rings, forming thin slats which could then be woven into strong baskets or backpacks. Ash grows quite rapidly, so the tree can actually be planted and harvested. This saves it from the fate of many other valuable hardwoods, which, being slow-growing and in great demand, do not replace themselves as quickly as they are methodically cut from within our forests.

Aspen (*Populus grandidentata, Populus tremuloides*)

Eroded mountainsides, neglected fields, burned-over forests, and turnpike cloverleafs are among the areas Aspens regularly grow in. Over time, Aspens have evolved adaptations which enable them to claim lands too remote or too poor in soil for other trees.

In spring, hundreds of thousands of Aspen seeds mature on the trees, each seed weighing less than a millionth of a pound. Their light weight enables them to be blown to remote areas; their abundance increases the chances of survival. The seeds, dispersing long before those of other trees, land on wet and open soil of spring, easily germinating and getting a head start on the competition for sunlight.

Aspen grove

Aspens are a member of the Poplar genus, which is part of the Willow family. As such, they put forth the familiar furry silver growths in late winter, just like the Pussy Willow.

*Aspen winter buds
and spring flowers*

These are actually flowers, the male and female flowers being borne on separate trees.

As young trees, Aspens grow rapidly reproducing by shoots from their roots as well as by seeds. The trees grow in dense stands that thin out with age. The stands rarely last more than eighty years, for the trees are very susceptible to attack by insects, bacteria, and fungi, and they do not thrive when shaded by taller trees.

Aspen wood is generally too weak and of small dimension to be useful as board lumber, but its abundance and rapid growth are in its favor. Today its main commercial uses are as pulpwood and as shredded wood to make fiberboard.

Aspen bark, though bitter, is the favorite food of Beavers, and after eating the bark they use the peeled, straight saplings in the construction of their dams and lodges. These

Aspen bark

peeled Aspen branches make light and sturdy walking sticks, and a beaver dam is a good place to collect one. Aspen bark and winter buds are also eaten by Grouse, Moose, Deer, and Rabbits.

Although Aspens in winter lack their refreshing summer leaves or their brilliant autumn color, they are still an inspiring sight, for the upper trunk and branches, now stripped of their foliage, reveal a light hue of green, which when increased by the dense stands, billows from forest edges like a spring haze.

Balsam Fir (*Abies balsamea*)

A sure way to identify Balsam Fir is to crush a few of its needles in your hand and smell them. If they give off a rich

Balsam Fir

pungent odor that somehow reminds you of Christmas, then you are standing next to a Balsam Fir. It may in fact be in your living room covered with ornaments, it may be a single small green tree in a deciduous forest, or it may be just one of many kinds of conifers packed into the dense northern woods.

Tolerant of shade, Balsam Fir keeps many of its lower branches, forming one of the most perfectly symmetrical evergreens. This shape, along with the fact that Balsam keeps its needles well after being cut, has made it a favorite species for Christmas trees. Over four million Balsam Firs are cut annually, along with millions of Spruces and Pines, just for use during Christmas. But since most of these are raised on tree farms, the huge market does not deplete our natural forests.

Like those of Hemlock, Balsam needles are flat and have rows of stomata, appearing as two white lines, on the underside of each needle. The needles tend to be shorter on the top branches than they are lower down, and they stay on the tree for as long as eight years before being shed. Grouse sit on Balsam branches and eat the needles, whereas Moose and Deer browse the whole twig. The canopy of Balsam's lower branches forms a protected place for animals and birds to stay during severe weather.

Fir trees produce upright cones that are purple when young. Unlike those of other Conifers the cones drop their

Balsam cones

scales and release their seeds, leaving just a spike on the branch where the scales and seeds were attached. The seeds

have a single wing and are dispersed by the wind if the Crossbills, Squirrels, and Chipmunks don't eat them first. Firs occasionally reproduce vegetatively, when the lowest branches become covered with forest litter and send down their own roots.

If you get close to the trunk of a Balsam Fir you will see swellings in the young bark. They are called resin blisters; when broken by pressure, they release a clear fluid called Canada Balsam. This fluid is used commercially to mount microscope slides and to glue optical equipment, for when dry it has the same optical properties as glass. During forest fires these resin blisters burst into flames, adding to the rapid destruction of the trees.

As you go farther north, more and more gift shops try to sell you cushions and dolls stuffed with Balsam's fragrant needles, but these curios are only the merest hint of the natural odor which on a warm day can fill the air of the northern woods with its sunned fragrance.

Basswood (*Tilia* species)

A feature of Basswood in fall and early winter is its ingenious aerodynamic seed. Hard and rounded, it is counterbalanced beneath a leafy wing which spins as the seed falls. As with the winged seeds of Pine, Ash, Maple, and Tulip Tree, its purpose is merely to slow the seed's fall, allowing

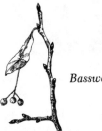

Basswood seeds

time for the wind to move it slightly away from the parent plant. This is in contrast to the parachuted seeds of Sycamore, Poplar, and Willow, which are actually caught up by the wind and carried great distances. In late winter, when the seeds are not present, Basswood can still be easily identified by its bright red waxy buds. The buds are each covered by two rounded scales. They are pleasant-tasting and produce a thick, syrupy mixture in your mouth.

Basswood

Many parts of Basswood trees are useful. The flowers can be dried and used for tea or for scenting bathwater. The inner bark, when soaked free from the outer bark, forms long fibrous strands, which can be twined into rope or woven into mats and fishnets. The wood is light in color and weight, and perhaps it's best known for its use in the forms that hold comb honey.

Basswood's tall trunk and arching branches create pleasant shade, and this property, along with its fragrant blossoms, has led it to be extensively planted in city parks and backyard lawns. In the wilds, the tree is most often an isolated one growing among other deciduous hardwoods.

Beech (*Fagus grandifolia*)

Groves of Beeches are at their best in winter, when sunlight reflecting off their smooth silver bark illuminates the forest space. On the younger trees, dried leaves often remain; drained of their green, they no longer catch the light, but

Beech trunks

they brighten as it passes through. In colonial times they were used to stuff mattresses, for they are long-lasting, springy, and softer than straw.

You, may see nut husks dotting the tree's upper branches, or littering the snow beneath. The four-part husk is prickly and, when young, encloses a delicious triangular nut. You can gather the nuts in fall, but you mustn't be late, for birds

Beech buds, husks, and nuts

and mammals soon strip them from the trees. A large crop of nuts is produced every two to three years.

Pure stands of Beeches are common. They are created because Beeches, like Hemlocks, are tolerant of shade and themselves cause shady conditions unfavorable to most other saplings. Also, mature Beeches send up shoots from their lateral roots, producing many saplings that take over when older trees die. Deer may also help create Beech stands, for they leave Beech saplings alone while heavily browsing the buds of other saplings, such as Oak, Maple, Ash, and Birch.

We are lucky that such a majestic tree as the Beech has proved itself relatively useless as commercial wood.

Birch (*Betula* species)

Birches are best known in winter by the horizontal markings on their tight-fitting bark. These markings, called lenticels, allow air to penetrate the bark into the inner growing layer

Birches

of the trunk. As Birches grow their bark fits more tightly, then stretches; the lenticels become stretched, and soon the pressure makes the bark peel off. The bark on each species of Birch peels differently: White Birch bark peels in large sheets of paper; Yellow Birch bark peels in small curling strips; and Sweet Birch bark hardly peels at all.

Birch bark is extremely durable and often lasts long after the wood has rotted away. Some small birds take advantage of this fact by pecking through the bark and hollowing out nest cavities in the rotted wood. Hollow cylinders of White Birch bark lying on the forest floor can be used as kindling for fires, the resin in them burning even after a heavy rain.

Look for catkins growing on the tips of the upper branches; they are small oblong growths occurring in one's, two's, or three's. In spring they will open and produce pollen to fertilize the female catkins. The clusters of seeds, which mature by fall, often last into winter. They are tightly

Birch seeds

packed into a conelike form; birds use them as a valuable winter food, and the wind disperses them over the snow's crust, making them appear like small stars in a snowy sky.

There are basically four Birches in the North. Two — White Birch and Gray Birch — have whitish bark. Gray Birch is also known as "Old-Field Birch" because of its habit of reforesting old abandoned fields. White Birch is also

White Birch bark   *Yellow Birch bark*

known as Paper Birch because of the quality of the bark, which can be written on and which peels off in large sections. These big pieces of bark were used by American Indians for canoes and by early settlers in their roofs. Yellow Birch has silvery bark, and its wood is the most valuable

Sweet Birch bark

commercially; it is favored for fine furniture because it is strong and takes a good finish. Sweet Birch has black bark and is named for the oil of wintergreen in its twigs. A mildly flavored tea can be made by steeping the young twigs in boiling water.

Birches are valuable winter food: Rabbits and Deer browse the twigs, Grouse eat the buds, and numerous small birds feast on the seeds.

Buckeye (*Aesculus* species)

At the tips of Buckeye's sinuous branches are the largest end buds of all our northern trees. Their upward pointing betrays the habit of the tree's lush flowers, which in late spring are borne on upright spikes. Inside the brown, shiny bud

Horsechestnut

you will also find miniature palmate compound leaves, five leaflets radiating from the tip of a single stem like the fingers of your hand (thus the word "palm"-ate). A sticky substance on the buds' surface may help protect them from

Buckeye bud

insect invasion. The side buds are opposite each other, making Buckeye one of our four trees with opposite buds.

Perhaps the most familiar feature of Buckeyes is their shiny mahogany-colored seeds. Normally three of these are produced in each green husk. When it drops in autumn, the husk splits into three parts, revealing the seeds. On each seed there is a round gray scar called the "hilum." It marks the place where nourishment was passed between the seed and the tree, and its shape reminded someone of a buck's eye — thus the tree's name. (Acorns also have conspicuous hila where they were attached to their caps.) The Buckeye seeds can be found beneath the tree during fall and winter thaws.

Although it is obviously rich in starch, the seed is rarely eaten by wildlife, possibly because it contains esculin, a glucoside (plant sugar) poisonous to most animals. People

Buckeye nut and husk

have been known to use the seeds for ground meal after extensive leaching in water, and I have noticed Squirrels peeling them, eating only the area around the hilum. Although inedible for humans, they certainly are attractive, so smooth to the touch and shiny to look at. It is hard to leave the tree without a few of them in your pocket.

There are at least three species of Buckeyes in the north. The Yellow Buckeye (*Aesculus octandra*) and Ohio Buckeye (*Aesculus glabra*) are two native trees that grow near the southern Great Lakes. Horsechestnut (*Aesculus hippocastanum*) is an alien member of the Buckeyes, native to Asia and introduced here from Europe. It is often planted as a shade tree and is now common in the eastern half of North America.

Cedar (*Juniperus virginiana, Thuja occidentalis*)

Neither Eastern Red Cedar nor Northern White Cedar is actually a Cedar, nor are they in the same genus. Nevertheless, they are often grouped together because of their names and outward similarity. Both are evergreens, are shaped like spires, and have small scalelike leaves distinct from those of our other evergreen trees. But this is where the similarity stops.

Red Cedars

Eastern Red Cedars, *Juniperus virginiana*, are sun-loving trees that soon die when overshadowed. Their small blue berries are eaten by mice and birds, which then disperse the seeds as undigested remains of their droppings. Therefore, Red Cedar is found scattered across fields where mice have runways and placed along fencerows where birds often perch. Once dispersed, the seeds take two or three years to germinate. Cedars grow slowly and are most often seen dotting the poorer soil of neglected fields.

The male and female "flowers" of Red Cedar are often on separate trees. The female flowers produce light blue fleshy cones, which look like berries and are fragrant when crushed. The cones last through fall, forming an important source of winter food. Grosbeaks, Finches, and various mice eat them; the Cedar Waxwing even gets its name from its love of the fruit.

The foliage of Red Cedars is of two kinds: square scales pressed close to the twig and short projecting sharp needles.

Red Cedar needles and berries

In open sunlight the foliage is dense and forms a thick cover for many animals. Mockingbirds, Sparrows, and Robins nest in its cover. These nests are then reused as winter homes for Deermice, which cover them over with soft plant fibers. The foliage is also excellent for roosting. Juncos or Sparrows may stay there during the night or through severe winter storms.

Red Cedars can live to be three hundred years old. Their longevity is usually explained by the resistance of their wood to insect attacks and fungal decay. The red wood has a fragrance familiar to those who have stored clothes in cedar chests or spread cedar chips in the bottom of a hamster cage. Pencils used to be made only with Red Cedar, but the tree is now so scarce that manufacturers have switched to the Western Incense Cedar.

Red Cedar is very susceptible to fire, for it has a shallow root system that is easily hurt by the heat, and its thin bark is very flammable. The bark, easily pulled from the tree in long thin wisps, makes an excellent kindling for campfires, and if only the outer layers are taken, the tree is not damaged. In the Northeast, Red Cedars are often found with large areas of their trunk bark shredded off. The culprits are Red Squirrels, which use the peeled bark to insulate the inner layer of their leafy nests.

In contrast to the Red Cedar, the Northern White Cedar, or Arborvitae (*Thuja occidentalis*), often forms dense stands, especially at the borders of swampy land. It is more common than Red Cedar in the North and an important member of the rich and varied northern conifer forests. Its foliage, rich green sprays of flattened scales, creates a dense form, shaped much like the spade on a deck of cards. The needles, when crushed, give off a strong pungent odor. White-tailed Deer browse these leaves and twigs so heavily that often the trees are trimmed clean as high as a deer can reach.

Arborvitae is also a slow-growing tree, but it has a tough fire-resistant bark that is easily distinguished from that of Red Cedar. Since the wood resists rotting and splits easily along growth rings, it is used for roof shingles. The Indians used to use it for the frames of their canoes.

Northern White Cedar

In further contrast with the Red Cedar, White Cedar has a cone with winged seeds. These cones are produced in

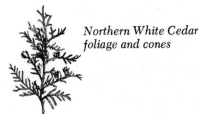

*Northern White Cedar
foliage and cones*

large numbers every three to five years, and are extensively eaten in winter by Finches.

Cherry (*Prunus* species)

Horizontal lenticels, so characteristic of Birches, are present on the bark of Cherry trees also. Cherries can be told from Birches in winter by the lack of catkins on their upper branches and by their straight rather than zigzag twigs.

Two other phenomena aid in identifying Cherry trees: the old webbed nests of leaf-eating caterpillars and a fungal distortion of the twigs. Both the Tent Caterpillar and Fall Webworm eat the leaves of Cherries, building protective webs as they do so. By winter these nests appear as disheveled masses of webbing, and from a distance they are often mistaken for birds' nests. The growth called Black Knot is also common; it appears as a black warty mass surrounding twigs or branches. It is caused by a fungus whose growth kills cells and distorts the branches.

Cherries vary widely in form, depending on their habitat. Reaching for sunlight within forests, they produce tall, branchless trunks, whereas in open fields their growth is stunted, the trunk dividing into many gnarled branches.

Cherry

There are basically three species of Cherries found in the area covered by this guide: Chokecherry, often only a shrub, favoring forest edges; Pin Cherry, which grows to 50 feet in height; and Wild Black Cherry, a forest tree, which grows the largest of the three.

Black Cherry bark

Wild Black Cherry is the woodworker's delight; its strong, fine-grained wood, with a red color that darkens with age and a surface that takes high-quality finishes, is rivaled among American hardwoods only by Black Walnut. Up to 1900, Cherry was still plentiful and used for common objects, but now the best lumber trees have been methodically cut from the forests, making good-sized Cherry trees scarce, so that Cherry wood is used only in expensive items.

*Black Cherry twig and
two Pin Cherry twigs*

In summer, Cherry trees produce hundreds of fruits, each usually with a large pit and thin layer of surrounding flesh. Birds, including Robins, Waxwings, Crossbills, and Grosbeaks, seem to cease all other eating habits in order to gorge themselves on the barely ripened fruit. The combination of a fruit so attractive to wildlife and the indigestible quality of the pit adds up to a foolproof method of seed dispersal. Birds fly away and disgorge the pits, while mammals excrete them in their feces. With varying amounts of work and sugar, the fruits of all three varieties of Cherries can be made into fine jams and preserves.

Dogwood, Flowering (*Cornus florida*)

The distinct and upturned flower buds on Dogwood in winter are a promise of the delicate, subtle beauty the tree puts out in spring, lining the borders between fields and woods with a fringe of white. Flowering Dogwood always favors these woodland margins as well as the understory of open forests. The tree is not as common in the North as most would wish it to be, being replaced by numerous shrubby relatives.

The flowers develop into bunches of red berries by late

Flowering Dogwood

fall, which are an important wildlife food, some of them lasting into the winter. Squirrels, Grouse, Turkeys, Cardinals, and Grosbeaks are the main northern consumers. The twigs and bark are eaten primarily by Rabbits.

The wood of the Flowering Dogwood is one of the hardest and heaviest woods in North America; it has the special quality of becoming very smooth with continued use. These qualities, plus the fact that the trees are rarely large enough for board lumber, created the custom of using Dogwood to

Dogwood leaf and flower buds

make shuttles for weaving. When weaving machines began to be used, Dogwood was even more valuable, for it could withstand the increased impact stress the machines inflicted on the shuttles. The same qualities made the wood useful for pulleys, sled runners, and hayforks. Today plastic shuttles and metal replace its former uses.

Elm (*Ulmus* species)

Few trees have as close an association with summer's ease as the American Elm; its tall trunk divides 20 feet above the ground into many large arching branches, providing a huge area of filtered shade as well as plenty of space beneath the

American Elm

tree in which to enjoy it. These features, along with the graceful sway of the Elm's branches, has earned it a place in thousands of parks and along even more town and city streets.

But actually there are two other Elms that do not have this form and are thus often neglected: they are the Rock, or Cork, Elm (*Ulmus thomasii*) and the Red, or Slippery, Elm (*Ulmus rubra*). Of the two the Slippery Elm has received more attention, because of the properties of its light-colored inner bark. This slippery but pleasant-smelling bark used to be stripped off the trees in spring, dried in the sun, and ground up. The powder was then applied to reduce inflammation from cuts and sores. The inner bark also was chewed.

The Cork Elm gets its common name from the corky ridges of bark that often run the length of its inner twigs.

Elm twigs and bark

The tree has markedly drooping branch tips. It is not common on the East Coast, but it is frequently found on uplands from Western New England into the Great Lakes area.

Elm seeds are an important early spring food for birds and squirrels. Deer eat the twigs and buds in winter. The strong pendant tips of Elm branches are a favorite spot for Orioles to construct their hanging nests.

Dead Elm

In the 1930s a fungus, already known in Europe as *Cera-tostomella ulmi*, found its way to this continent. It grew on Elms, killing them, and came to be known as Dutch elm disease. It is spread by a native engraver beetle, which feeds on Elms. As the beetle flies to new trees, it carries the fungal spores with it, facilitating their entry into the wood by its own habits of boring holes through the bark. Despite attempts to stop the fungus, it spread rapidly and wiped out thousands of Elms throughout the continent. Since Elm was the only planted tree on the streets of many towns in New England, the disease had a particularly devastating effect on these streets — once covered and kept cool by grand arcades of Elms, now bare and baked by the summer sun.

So common are the dead or dying trees that a particular woody mushroom, *Polyporus conchifer*, that lives on them has also become common. It is pure white and about the size and shape of a bottle cap. You can often find it on a fallen twig on the sidewalk, and in that setting it is like a symbol, pointing to both the Elm's popularity among humans and the wild tree's potential extinction.

Hawthorn (*Crataegus* species)

The word "haw" is Anglo-Saxon for "fence" or "hedge" and is certainly well placed in the name of Hawthorns, for not

Hawthorns

only have the trees been used for centuries in Europe as hedges between fields, but they also tend to grow along fences, for birds void the seeds there after eating the bright red berries. The tree also typically grows in old fields because of further distribution by birds.

What makes Hawthorns valuable as hedges are their strong and dangerously sharp thorns, which line the branches. Birds find the trees ideal for nesting, well protected from Raccoons, Squirrels, snakes, and other egg eaters. Why some trees develop thorns and others don't is certainly a good question. Thorns don't protect the berries from birds, nor do they keep Rabbits from eating the bark, Deer from browsing on the twigs, or insects from eating the leaves. Thorns would keep Squirrels, Raccoons, and other

Thorns and Rabbit-chewed bark of Hawthorn

medium-sized mammals from climbing the tree for the berries or leaves, but this is about all. Thorns may have evolved when the tree had different needs and may now remain simply as a vestige.

There are hundreds of varieties of Hawthorns in eastern North America. There is a great deal of variety in the taste and quality of Hawthorn berries; some are considered edible right off the tree, others, by far the majority, inedible. In any case, it is commonly agreed that most, when boiled down and sweetened, make some of our best wild fruit jellies and marmalades.

Hemlock (*Tsuga canadensis*)

Hemlocks are shade-loving trees, often found on north-facing slopes along river gorges. In mature stands, they create such dense shade that only their own seedlings can

Hemlock

survive. These groves remain nothing but Hemlocks until man, disease, or fire alters their condition enough to enable other trees to invade. This is one type of climax forest — a forest that will normally regenerate itself and will not allow the invasion of new plant types.

The underside of every Hemlock needle is marked with two white lines, composed of hundreds of tiny openings into the leaf. These openings, called stomata, close and open as they regulate the flow of air and water vapor in and out of the leaf. All leaves have stomata, but in Hemlock they are grouped in such a way as to be visible.

Hemlock trees are not what poisoned Socrates. There are

a number of unrelated plants of the carrot family, also called Hemlock, which are highly poisonous, but this tree's buds and needles are edible, and although not very tasty, can be used to make a weak tea. Grouse and Rabbits eat these buds and needles; Deer also strip young saplings of their greenery, depending on it as a winter staple when other food is covered by snow.

Hemlock cones are another source of wildlife food. Growing at the ends of twigs, they are less than 1 inch long and contain two winged seeds under each of their scales. They open in dry, cold weather and close at other times. Both Red Squirrels and Deermice chew off the scales to get at the

Hemlock needles   Hemlock cones

seeds; the Red Squirrel scatters the scales as it eats, while the Deermouse leaves them in a neat little pile on the snow. Many birds depend on the seeds for food in winter.

A common winter resident in Hemlock trees in certain localities is the Porcupine. It may climb a Hemlock and stay there for weeks, eating the bark and chewing off large twigs. These twigs strewn over the snow are a sure sign of the animal's presence; they are also valuable to Deer as winter browse which they otherwise could never have reached.

Because Hemlocks like shade, their lower branches live for many years. Even after they die they remain on the tree, collecting sap where they join the trunk. These pitch knots are so hard they can chip saw blades, making many Hemlocks useless as lumber.

In the 1800s Hemlock bark furnished the raw material for an entire industry. It contains great amounts of tannin, an oil used to tan leather. Large 4-foot squares were stripped off the trees, girdling them and causing them to die. Since Pine, which was abundant, was a more service-able wood, Hemlocks were left to rot by the hundreds of acres. Today, with the development of synthetic tanning agents, Hemlock bark is no longer used.

Hickory (*Carya* species)

The most distinctive and prevalent Hickory is the Shagbark. Its trunk bark splits off in large, gray arcs, making the tree clearly shaggy in appearance. Once you have seen it, there is no mistaking it thereafter.

Shagbark Hickory

The forces that cause its bark to split are common to all trees. Trees grow new bark under the old, pushing it outward. Every species of tree reacts differently to this outward pressure, depending on the structure of its bark. Shagbark

Shagbark Hickory bark

Hickory sloughs off its outer bark at a very young age and in larger pieces than any of our other northern trees. Its common name is obviously well chosen.

There are basically four types of Hickories in the area of this guide: Shagbark, Pignut, Mockernut, and Bitternut, each having a distinctive end bud and all having large shield-shaped leaf scars. As their names imply, they all produce nuts. These nuts are characteristically enclosed in a four-part husk, which splits when the nut is ripe, unlike walnuts, which have a leathery husk which doesn't split. The smooth shell of Hickory nuts varies in thickness with the different species, Shagbark having the thinnest shell as well as a tasty and edible nut. The other species are thick-shelled, so they are less valuable to wildlife.

*Shagbark Hickory bud
and leaf stem*

*Shagbark Hickory
nut and husk*

Perhaps one of the best-known uses of Hickory wood is in smoke-curing ham products such as bacon and ham. The green, unseasoned wood is used, but the dry, seasoned wood is also an excellent fuel wood, and it is claimed that a cord of Hickory is equal to a ton of coal in the amount of heat energy it can produce.

Hop Hornbeam (*Ostrya virginiana*)

Hop Hornbeam is probably a tree name that few have heard of before, yet the tree is common in the areas included in this guide. It usually grows as an isolated tree under the canopy of taller Maples, Beeches, and Birches,

Hop Hornbeam

and is easy to recognize by its bark and small size. The bark is composed of thin rectangular overlapping strips, slightly curving outward at their bottom ends.

Also distinctive on the tree in winter are its male flowers,

Hop Hornbeam bark

called catkins. Their presence shows the tree's relationship to Birches, which also have winter catkins, although Birch bark is very different from that of Hop Hornbeam. In spring the catkins release pollen, fertilizing the female catkins. Hop Hornbeam's unusual seed cases develop in the fall and look somewhat like Hops — thus that part of the tree's name.

Hop Hornbeam seeds and catkins

The seeds are encased in separate light tan envelopes and dispersed by being blown across the snow's surface.

Although the wood is one of the hardest and strongest known, the tree is never large or common enough to be used for its wood. The seeds are also too few to be of value to wildlife.

Hop Hornbeam is a beautiful tree in winter; its finely divided bark, dark red twigs, and lanternlike seed casings that ornament the lower branches always make it a rewarding find in the winter woods.

Hornbeam (*Carpinus caroliniana*)

Between the canopy of leaves formed by tall hardwood trees and the shrub layer that is close to the forest floor is the understory. It is an ecological niche to which the American Hornbeam is perfectly adapted. It loves moist soil, and its trunk branches freely close to the ground, forming a crown that is flat-topped and spreading. This branching pattern distributes its leaves laterally so that they can make the most of the dappled light that filters through the forest canopy.

Hornbeam bark

This understory, also filled in with Dogwoods and shade-tolerant saplings of other trees, is a protected environment — sheltered from the heat and drying action of the sun,

Hornbeam seeds and twigs

from pelting rainstorms, and from wind. It is an ideal place for birds' nests and insect development; it also provides berries, seeds, browse, and leaves for mammals, birds, and insects.

Hornbeam, Birch, and Hop Hornbeam all belong to the Birch family (*Betulaceae*). They have similar twigs, but the seeds and bark of all three are very different. Hornbeam seeds are in a cluster, each having its own wing, like those of Maple seeds. Its bark, hard and smooth, lacks the horizontal lenticels of Birch and the vertical strips of Hop Hornbeam, and of the three it is the only one without catkins in winter.

Larch (*Larix laricina*)

All summer, the Larches have looked like evergreens, covered from top to bottom with bunches of soft gray-green needles. But in fall the trees turn a golden yellow and drop all their needles as if they had been hit by a blight. Since we are used to coniferous (cone-bearing) trees being evergreen, the Larch looks dead — but it's not. The Larch is our one deciduous (leaf-shedding) coniferous tree.

The needles in summer grow in bunches out of stubby twigs similar to the fruit spurs of Apple trees. These spurs are very visible in winter, so they make identification easy. The small cones, when they have opened to release seeds, look like woody flowers, growing upright along the branches.

Larch displays an ordered pattern of growth in winter. It has a single excurrent (undivided) trunk off which grow

Larch grove

long shoots, the main structural branches. Off these grow short shoots, the fillers, and off these the spurs and then the needles. Excurrent growth makes it well suited for lumber. Larch is durable, too, when in contact with earth or water.

Larch twigs with spars and cones

It has been commercially used for posts, railroad ties, doorsills, and boat keels.

In the coniferous forests of the northern woods, Larches often form tight groves, especially around moist, boggy areas. As winter comes and they drop their needles, these groves seem like holes or vacuums in the dense fabric of the impenetrable evergreens.

Locust (*Robinia pseudoacacia, Gleditsia triacanthos*)

Even though they are not directly related, Honey Locust and Black Locust are grouped together here, because they are the only arboreal (tree) members of the Legume family in the area of this guide. Legumes are mainly characterized by their production of pods containing seeds. Of course, all

Black Locust

of the vegetables we call beans are in the Legume family, too. The pods of Black Locust are 3 to 4 inches long and

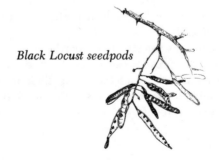

Black Locust seedpods

contain 4 to 8 small black, poisonous seeds. The pods of
Honey Locust are up to 18 inches long and have large
round seeds surrounded by a sweet-tasting gummy pith.
The pods of both Locusts hang on the trees in winter, the
Black Locust pods lasting till spring, the Honey Locust pods
littering the ground on early winter. Black Locust is insignifi-
cant as wildlife food, and Honey Locust pods and seeds are
eaten only by cattle and a few squirrels.

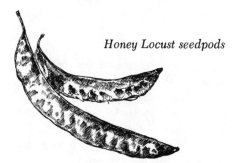

Honey Locust seedpods

The Black Locust is very important, however, as a re-
claimer of strip-mined areas and other ravaged land. Its
extensive fibrous root system and ability to send up suckers
after its first five years of growth enable it to hold run-off
water effectively and prevent erosion. It also attracts certain
bacteria, which, in cooperation with the roots, absorb nitrogen from the air within the soil and incorporate it into the
plant matter. This is an important process for all living
things, for although nitrogen is the major constituent of the
atmosphere and an essential part of every protein and
amino acid, we, along with most higher plants and animals,
have no way of directly absorbing nitrogen, so we depend
on these bacteria to absorb nitrogen and make it available
to plants, which in turn make it available to us.

In the process of absorbing nitrogen, the Black Locust
rejuvenates soil in which nitrogen compounds have been
leached away. Honey Locust, however, does not have this
ability.

Both of these trees have scientific names that honor fa-

Honey Locust trunk thorns

mous botanists associated with them. Both were named by Linnaeus around 1750, *Robinia* for Jean and Vespasien Robin, who had been botanical explorers for the kings of France in the previous century and who introduced Black Locust into Europe, *Gleditsia* for Johann Gottlieb Gleditsch, a well-known botanist in Germany at the time of Linnaeus.

Both Locusts have spines, but you have to look closely to see the small, often opposite, thorns on Black Locust twigs. The thorns on Honey Locust are huge and forked, covering the branches and often lining the trunk in a gruesome manner.

Maple (*Acer* species)

Almost every part of the Maple is used by wildlife as food. Beavers and Porcupines chew the bark. Rabbits and Hares, Deer and Moose browse the twigs and winter buds. Buds as well as flowers are eaten by Grosbeaks, Purple Finches, Nuthatches, and Grouse; and the seeds are stripped of their wings and stored as winter food by Squirrels and Chipmunks. Besides these food uses, the stalks of the seeds and leaves are used by birds in the construction of their nests.

As food for people, the Maples are not half as productive, but what they do produce is well-known to people of all ages. It is, of course, maple sugar and syrup, made from the

*Sugar Maples with
maple syrup buckets*

spring-rising sap. The sap is water absorbed by the roots and mixed with some of the stored sugars of the trees. Sap runs best on warm days that are preceded by freezing nights; depending on the latitude, these conditions can occur at any time from the first of the year to late spring.

It was the American Indians who first taught the early settlers about taking sap from trees. Since water from the roots travels up the outer portion of the trunk, a hole ½ inch in diameter must be drilled 3 inches into the tree. The hole must slant downward, so that the sap will flow out. A short length of pipe is placed snugly in the hole, and a bucket is hung beneath it. An average tree can easily feed two taps; they will release more than 20 gallons of sap in one spring. That amount will boil down to about two quarts of syrup, and, with more boiling, about 3 or 4 pounds of sugar. All maples can produce good sap in some quantity; there is as much variation in sugar content within one species as there is between species. Even so, 90 percent of the trees tapped are Sugar Maples.

Maple lumber is traditionally divided into two types:

hard maple, from Sugar and Black Maples, and soft maple, from Red and Silver Maples. The hard Maples are by far the most important commercially. Wood from Sugar Maple is even lighter, stronger, and stiffer than that of White Oak, and has been used extensively since early colonial times for tools, furniture, floors, and musical instruments. Some Sugar Maples have a curving grain which produces the highly prized bird's-eye, or curly, maple. Wood of the soft Maple group is less resilient and splits easily, so it is not used commercially.

Red Maples

The most common Maple of eastern and central northern America is the Red Maple. Thriving in low swampy areas and near lakes and streams, it often forms pure stands. It is well-named, for in early spring it puts forth clusters of red flowers followed by leaves with red stems; then in fall the leaves turn a brilliant scarlet and, after dropping, reveal red twigs and red leaf and flower buds. Their color lasts all winter and somehow symbolizes a promise of their blooming and the distant return of spring.

Oak (*Quercus* species)

No other tree provides as much for as many as do the Oaks. Their rich fall harvest of acorns feeds many of our north-

Oak

ern animals. Most birds, including the Ruffed Grouse, Blue Jay, Nuthatch, and Titmouse, just eat the nut after pecking open the shell, but the Wild Turkey eats them whole, consuming up to 50 in one meal. Large mammals such as Bears, Deer, and Raccoons also depend on acorns in winter, but the real consumers are the Squirrels. The Red, Gray, and Fox Squirrels all store tremendous hoards of acorns in the fall as winter reserves. The Gray Squirrel's habit of burying nuts singly and forgetting to eat some of them places the

Acorns

seeds in a perfect position for germination, protected from freezing in winter, and planted a few inches under the soil. It is suspected that a considerable number of our northern Oaks have grown from plantings such as these.

Numerous kinds of insects also find food and protection within the Oaks. Insects produce over 300 types of Oak galls, many easily seen in winter on the buds, twigs, and dead leaves. Looking like a tan Ping-Pong ball, the Oak Apple Gall hangs on the tree through the winter. It is made on the vein of a leaf by a wasp. Bullet Galls are another common winter sight — small, hard, gray spheres attached to the new twigs. (See Chapter 4.)

Young Oak with dried leaves remaining on it

While living Oaks are quite resistant to fungi, dead Oaks are havens for the hungry roots of wood-destroying fungi. Dead trunks and isolated limbs are frequently lined with the colorful concentric rings of the Turkey Tail fungus, or the purple gills of *Polyporus pergamenus*, or the mazelike pattern of *Daedalia quercina*. (See Chapter 6.)

Where Oak limbs fall off, insects and fungi eat into the heartwood, forming soft cavities. These are then hollowed out by Woodpeckers searching for insects or making nests. After being abandoned by the Woodpecker, these holes are reused either by other birds such as Owls, Starlings, and Chickadees, or by Squirrels as their winter home.

We also have come to the Oak for many of these same reasons. The Indians harvested the acorns to grind into flour; the early settlers used the galls and bark to make ink and dyes, while also using the bark's tannic acid to tan leather. And of course, to this day, the wood of the Oak has been one of our most valued and durable, extensively used for boats, floors, barrels, tools, and furniture.

The Oak, whether living or dead, seems to attract life to itself by its ability to produce food and homes for a large range of living things, from humans to animals to birds to insects to fungi.

Pine (*Pinus* species)

The Pine is one of the first seed-bearing trees to have evolved; pines existed before the age of dinosaurs. Today they grow in many parts of North America, their form relatively unchanged for over 250 million years. This consistency is due to a flexibility in adaptation that has enabled

Pines

Pines to survive the changing climates and natural catastrophes that are so much a part of geologic time.

Their needle-shaped leaves are among their adaptations. Minimized surface area and wax coating cut down on evaporation and shed the weight of snow, helping the tree to survive in cold climates. The needles stay on the trees for 3 to 5 years and are replaced by new ones that grow at the tips of the branches.

Some species of Pine have adapted in relation to fire. The

Pitch Pine cone and seeds

White and Red Pines both have a thick outer bark, which insulates the sensitive growth cells within the trunk from the killing heat. The Jack Pine, and to a lesser extent the Pitch Pine, produces cones that remain closed and on the tree for many years. Only after the extreme heat of a forest fire will the Jack Pine open its cone and release its seeds. They fall on the open burned land and establish themselves before most other trees do. In this way, large stands of Jack Pine have developed around the western Great Lakes.

White Pine needles and cones

Pitch Pine needles and cones

The growth of Pines is termed "excurrent," which means that small branches grow off the sides of a single central trunk. Excurrent growth is controlled by a dominant terminal bud at the top of the trunk. Through the release of plant growth hormones, called auxins, this bud regulates the lower growth of the tree. When the apical bud is injured, as by lightning or insects, the nearest side branch or branches will turn upward and resume the function of the apical bud. This distortion is a common occurrence in Pines; look for a trunk split into two main parts, or one with a sharp curve. There is an insect, the White Pine Weevil, that attacks the apical bud of White Pines. It is considered a real pest by lumbermen, who are looking for the straight wood normal excurrent growth produces.

Pine branches grow in whorls around the trunk, in many species, one group for each year of development. In forest growth, only the upper branches stay alive; the lower ones die back, breaking off near the trunk.

Among trees, Pines are second only to Oaks in providing

Jack Pine needles and cones

food for wildlife. In the northeastern quarter of the continent, the White Pine is most important in terms of food production. Numerous birds — including Chickadees, Crossbills, Grosbeaks, Nuthatches, and Siskins — feed on the nutritious seeds. Small mammals that eat the seeds are the Chipmunk, Red and Gray Squirrels, and the White-footed Mouse. Large mammals such as the Rabbit, Porcupine, Beaver, and Deer tend to eat only the bark and foliage.

The Pines are trees of pleasant sensations: the soft mat of their fallen needles, the faint smell of their resin in the sun, and the whistling of the wind through their topmost branches. Perhaps because of their picturesque form, evergreen color, or continued usefulness to humans, Pines have become a special tree in myths and legends. They are a symbol for the unchanging aspects of life.

Poplar (*Populus* species)

There are four main trees in the north that belong to the Poplar genus: Aspen, Eastern Cottonwood, Balsam Poplar, and Lombardy Poplar. Aspens have been described separately because of their prevalence, importance, and distinctive winter buds. What the other three have in common are the size and shape of their winter buds, their flowers borne on catkins, and the male and female flowers growing on separate trees. After these similarities, they are so distinct in habit that it is better to deal with them individually.

Balsam Poplar buds

The Eastern Cottonwood, *Populus deltoides*, gets its common name from the cottony fluff that surrounds its seeds and seems to fill the spring air wherever the trees are plenti-

Balsam Poplar

ful. Cottonwoods inhabit a niche similar to that of Willows, growing along streambanks and spreading roots toward the water. They are a fast-growing tree and are harvested for pulpwood, packing crates, and veneer. Early settlers and pioneers frequently settled or camped near Cottonwoods in the Midwest, for the trees provided shelter from weather as well as firewood for themselves and browse for their livestock. Although the wood warps as it seasons, it was good for constructing temporary homes.

The Balsam Poplar, *Populus balsamifera*, loves the cold, growing farther north than any of our other native deciduous trees. It is similar to Aspens in shape and growth habits, but differs in one delectable way: its winter buds, when rubbed, give off a strange, deep scent, like some sweet oriental incense. It is a real treat to come across and I never

Lombardy Poplar

leave it without carrying away some of its fragrance in my lungs.

The Lombardy Poplar, *Populus nigra* of the variety *italica*, was originally imported from Italy, where it forms a characteristic part of the landscape. It is extensively used in landscaping, its tall spire of leaves providing an interesting form and a touch of greenery while not creating shade. The tree is also planted in long rows to act as windbreaks in open farming areas.

A strange aspect of this species is that only its male form is known, an identical tree with female flowers never having been found. Since it cannot be reproduced by seed, it is either planted from cuttings or from the suckers that spring up from its roots.

Sassafras (*Sassafras albidum*)

Don't leave Sassafras without tasting the bark of its distinctive green twigs; it has a sweet lime flavor. In fact, just about every part of this tree has either a pleasant smell or taste. The leaves in summer and fall taste much like the

Sassafras buds

winter twigs, the wood has a pleasant odor, and the outer bark of the roots reminds one of old-time root beer.

These odors and tastes impressed early European explorers of North America, giving them hope of the discovery of a new wonder medicine. Exaggerated reports began to get back to Europe, and by 1625 there was a large profitable market for the import of Sassafras roots as well as the lumber. Although it was, and still is, used to make a rich-tasting tea, its powers as a panacea soon came into question and the demand for Sassafras diminished accordingly.

The aromatic wood is durable and was believed to repel insects. This led to its being used for floorboards, storage

Sassafras clone

barrels, and bed frames. There is little or no use of Sassafras lumber today.

Sending up new saplings from the parent rootstock, Sassafras often forms whole groves. In a group of this kind every member is identical in gene content to the parent plant, since no sexual reproduction has taken place; groups of this kind are called *clones*.

Male and female Sassafras flowers grow on separate trees. When these are in the same area, the female flowers are fertilized and produce a hard blue fruit in the fall. Neither the fruits nor the leaves are a significant source of wildlife food, although the twigs and buds are occasionally eaten by deer and the fruits eaten by birds.

Spruce (*Picea* species)

After a storm the accumulation of snow under a stand of Spruce is only half that of deciduous forests. For Spruce trees, because of the placement of the needles, hold more snow on their branches than any other tree. The dense foliage of Spruce forests also lessens the full force of winds. These two factors cause many mammals to stay near Spruce groves during winter, for they provide warmth and freedom of movement in the shallow snow. Animals especially at-

Spruces

tracted to them are Deer, Snowshoe Hares, Bobcats, Lynx, and Fishers. Grouse roost in the trees, and small birds and Red Squirrels feed on the seeds.

To distinguish Spruce from Hemlock and Fir in the wild, simply take a bough in your hand and turn it over. If the underside is not distinctly lighter in color than the top side,

Red Spruce needles and cones

then it is Spruce. If it *is* distinctly lighter, then the tree is Hemlock or Fir. The needles of Black Spruce (*Picea mariana*) were once used in brewing a backwoods beer, and those of White Spruce (*Picea glauca*) have a bad odor when crushed. Spruce needles remain on the tree for 7 to 10 years.

Red Spruce grows fastest of the three types in the northern area and is the most valuable commercially. Its long wood fibers make it an important paper pulp tree, and large tracts of Spruce Forests in North America are owned by paper companies. One specialized use of Spruce is for the sounding boards of musical instruments. If it is especially clear of knots and imperfections it resonates better than other woods.

Sycamore (*Platanus occidentalis*)

The Sycamore, best known for the mottled appearance of its bark, is the most massive American tree east of the Rockies.

Sycamore bark

In the open it produces a huge crown, over 100 feet across, with large branches spreading low and parallel to the ground. It grows in rich bottomlands, often lining the banks of rivers and streams.

Although Sycamore wood is hard, it has a tendency to rot inside the trunk, leaving the tree supported by just the outer layer of the trunk. Such hollows are ideal homes for animals such as Opossums, Raccoons, and Skunks, as well as for hibernating Bats, or day-resting Swallows. The outside trunks of some of the largest trees enclosed empty areas of up to 125 square feet, the size of a regular bedroom, and Sycamores of this size were used by early settlers as barns and even as homes.

Sycamore also has the largest leaf of all our deciduous trees with simple leaves. Since the tree is also particularly resistant to smoke and exhaust fumes, Sycamore is good for planting as a city shade tree.

Seed clusters, called buttonballs, hang on the tips of its zigzag branches in winter. Each is a spherical packing of over 200 seeds around a hard central core. The seeds are

Sycamore seed balls

slightly conical, and each has its own parachute of filaments. In winter the buttonballs break apart and the seeds float to the ground or onto the water, where they are carried to new muddy areas suitable for growth.

The wood of the Sycamores, when not rotted, is fairly light, tough, and hard to split. It has been used in the past for dugout canoes, solid wagon wheels, boxes, furniture, and butchers' blocks. The hollow trunks of branches were also used as barrels; one simply cut a length and nailed a bottom on it.

The Sycamore is one of the loveliest trees in the winter

Sycamore

woods, easily recognized by the marvelous rounded shapes of green, white, and tan created by the peeling of its inelastic bark. Unfortunately, the tree needs rich soils to grow on, and humans continually cleared those soils for farming. So now the Sycamore, although common in the cities, is less often found in its native habitat and seldom grows to the immense size of its ancestors.

Tulip Tree (*Liriodendron tulipifera*)

The Tulip Tree grows to be one of the tallest broadleaf trees in eastern North America. In forests, it produces a straight trunk free of branches for most of its height. This straightness and lack of branches, along with wood that is light, strong, and easily worked, have made it a valuable lumber tree.

Tulip Tree

The Tulip Tree is a member of the Magnolia family and as such has beautiful, large blossoms in early summer. These develop into seeds with attached wings, arranged on the twigs like the petals of a flower. They are one of the best signs by which you can identify the tree, for they last into winter, their light beige color shining out into the sunlight. But to get a closer look at them, you may need binoculars, because of the height of the tree. What little value these seeds have as wildlife food is due mainly to their being present in winter.

Another good way to recognize the winter tree is by its flattened end buds. They are shaped like a duck's bill, and the twig adjacent to them tastes at first like Sassafras, then seems slightly bitter.

Tulip Tree seed clusters

The Greek genus name, *Liriodendron*, means "lily tree," and the species name, *tulipifera*, means "tulip-bearing." Linnaeus, when he named this tree, was obviously emphasizing the tulip-shaped leaves and the large summer blossoms, and maybe even the flowerlike design of the winter seeds.

Walnut (*Juglans* species)

If you come upon a Walnut tree, consider yourself lucky, for it is rare to find one growing naturally in the woods and more common to find Walnut trees growing around houses

White Walnut

Black Walnut nuts,
some opened by Squirrels

or in city parks. Before white settlers arrived, the Walnuts were common in our deciduous forests, and the American Indians used the nuts for food and the husks for dye. But the European settlers, discovering the great qualities of the wood, methodically cut almost all Walnuts from northeastern North America. The tree should now probably be protected by law.

There are two Walnuts native to this area: Black Walnut, *Juglans nigra,* and Butternut, *Juglans cinerea.* Black Walnut ranges farther south than Butternut, is the more valuable lumber tree, for it produces a tall massive trunk, and has dark heartwood, which turns a rich red-brown when oiled. The tree must be 20 to 30 years old before it produces walnuts, and even then good crops occur only every third year. The nuts of Black Walnut may be found beneath the tree in winter; they are round and about 1½ inches in diameter. The husk is leathery and has no divisions, unlike the Hickory nut husk, which is woody and comes off in four parts. The meat of the Black Walnut is hard to extract but well worth the effort; in fact usually you will find that a forest rodent has already taken the effort, leaving the shell behind.

Butternuts are so named because of the oil that can be extracted by boiling the split nuts in hot water. The oil and the nutmeats float to the top and, scraped off and mashed together, they can be used as a vegetable butter. The husks of both types of Walnut contain a yellow-brown stain that can be used as a dye. Butternut has also been called White Walnut, for its heartwood is a lighter color than that of Black Walnut. Butternuts, however, are typically short-trunked, spreading trees that are not as suitable for long-dimension lumber. Because they are spared cutting, the trees are more common, but their fruit is still often neglected.

White Walnut twig and buds

The leaf scars of both kinds of Walnut tree are large. A large leaf scar is usually left by a large or long leaf that needs extra support. The Walnuts have the largest compound leaf of our northern trees; its main stalk is 1 to 2 feet long, bearing from 11 to 23 leaflets. The Butternut is particularly easy to recognize by its twigs, for it has a furry "moustache" between its leaf scar and leafbud.

Willow (*Salix* species)

Willows are especially well adapted to colonizing the edges of streams and rivers. Their seeds, carried by the slow-moving water, will germinate in less than 2 days when washed up on a muddy bank. After germinating the plant may grow to a height of 7 feet during the first year, while at the same time developing an extensive fibrous root system. This rapid and extensive growth insures its survival in the variable and easily eroded environment of river edges. Besides seeds, the mature tree produces flexible twigs that break off easily from the main branch. If these break off during floods and later wash up on muddy banks downstream, they quickly sprout roots and start new trees.

For many years Willows have been planted by humans to control erosion and preserve the banks of waterways. Only

Black Willow

one Willow of tree size is native to our North: the Black Willow, *Salix nigra*. It is the largest of the Willows and has upward-pointing, orange twigs grouped at the ends of its branches. The twigs of other Willow trees are yellower and hang downward, like those of the Weeping Willow, *Salix*

Weeping Willow

babylonica, a native of China. Both of these trees are often planted near farm ponds or park lakes for their graceful summer foliage.

Like Dogwoods, the Willow genus has many species that are shrubs in the North; and also like Dogwood, these shrubs have buds that are distinctive and similar to those of the tree variety. These Willow shrubs often dominate the moist land surrounding meadow streams, forming dense,

Weeping Willow buds with single scale covering each

impenetrable thickets. Some of the most beautiful insect galls, such as the Willow Petaled Gall and Willow Pine Cone Gall, are formed on these shrubs. The best known of these shrubs is, of course, the Pussy Willow, *Salix discolor,* which is collected in late winter for its attractive furry flowers.

IV

Evidence of Insects

I HAVE ALWAYS THOUGHT that one of winter's strongest points was its lack of "bugs." Not bothered by mosquitoes, black flies, gnats, or ticks, I could go where I wanted; I was free to explore the swamp and no longer had to avoid the river's edge. And yet it was the "bugless" winter that first introduced me to insects. While exploring the winter woods, I saw more and more evidence of their summer feeding and winter homes. With the leaves gone, I saw insect tunnels in trees and insect homes in plant galls, and the marvelous nests of wasps and hornets could be explored without danger. The evidence of insects in winter is everywhere — on plants and buildings, in fields and woods, in city and country. Once spotted, it becomes increasingly evident, and the closer one looks the more one can learn about the habits and life histories of its makers.

One of the dominating facts in the study of insects is the tremendous diversity of the class. There are nearly one million species of insects now known and up to five thousand new species discovered each year. Because there are so many, we can't approach them as we do birds or mammals. The names and habits of all the larger mammals of a given area can be easily known. But considerably more effort would be needed to recognize even one hundredth of the local insect species. Clearly our emphasis must change from the species level to that of orders and families, and even then we are dealing with staggering numbers. The life histories of these insects are extremely diverse, yet some generalizations can be made which can help create a framework for further knowledge.

One such generalization, essential for any understanding of insects, concerns their stages of development. Unlike mammals, which have generally the same appearance all through their lives (if you know what a squirrel looks like you can recognize it whether it's young or old), insects undergo radically different stages in their lives. Some have as many as four stages, each distinct from the others in appearance. Other insects have a gradual development, which from beginning to end changes greatly but in which each consecutive stage is only slightly different from the one before and the one after.

In the latter type of metamorphosis (transformation), called *gradual*, the insect starts as an egg. Then a series of growth stages take place, in which the young insect molts its skin, becoming larger and slightly different with each molt. During the changing stages the insect is called a *nymph*, so gradual metamorphosis can be summarized as egg–nymph stages–adult. In the adult stage, the insect no longer molts; it is involved in reproducing.

The other type of development is known as *complete* metamorphosis; it consists first of the egg stage, from which hatches a small caterpillar or grub, known as the *larva*. The larva spends all its time eating food and growing, then it forms a coating (a pupa or cocoon) around itself and slowly changes into an adult. This is called the *pupal stage*. When the insect leaves this stage, it is an adult. So, complete metamorphosis can be summarized as egg–larva–pupa–adult.

Complete metamorphosis is considered the more recent type, and the majority of our insects undergo it, including moths, butterflies, wasps, bees, ants, and beetles. Bugs, dragonflies, crickets, and grasshoppers tend to have gradual metamorphosis.

But where are insects in winter? What do they do, where do they go, and why aren't we bothered by them?

All insects are cold-blooded. This designation simply means that their bodies are not internally regulated to a constant temperature; their temperature is generally that of their surroundings. Colder weather slows them down, and winter temperatures bring most of them to a standstill. In order to survive thermal changes, insects have adapted so that during the cold period of our temperate climate they enter a resting stage, in which they cease their life activities and development, until spring, when they reemerge and continue their development. This stage is called *diapause;* it occurs also in insects that experience dry and wet seasons. In general, diapause occurs during any season that is harsh to the normal activities of insects.

A good question is: what triggers the onset of diapause? Clearly, if an insect merely waited for the weather to get cold, it might be slowed down to the point where it could not complete its preparation for winter. It must prepare for winter while conditions are still good, long before the cold and the lack of food set in.

During the last hundred years it has slowly become apparent that many insects are sensitive to light and that their preparation for diapause is controlled by the changing ratio of day to night in late summer and fall. In the laboratory, caterpillers that normally build cocoons in late summer have been kept in their active feeding stage for up to 10 years by artificial lengthening of the day. Aphids that give birth to live young all summer but in fall change to laying eggs can be kept in their summer habits. Time and again light-to-dark ratios have been shown to be the starter of winter preparations in insects.

Preparation for diapause is generally accomplished in either or both of two ways. One is apparently intended to minimize the effect of the harsh environmental conditions. To do this many insects migrate, not north to south like birds but up to down; from the above-ground environment of trees, shrubs, and plants to areas beneath the ground, such as roots, fallen logs, rock crevices, burrows, or under leaf litter. Other insects migrate from above water to below it, still others go from shallow to deep water. In all cases, the winter environment is warmer and more stable than the air.

The other way an insect may prepare for diapause is to enter a different life stage, one that will best enable it to survive the winter. For many insects, this means the egg stage. Many adults lay their eggs in late summer and fall, and then die. The eggs start their development again in the spring and then hatch. Other insects are in the larval stage as caterpillars or grubs in summer and fall, feeding on the abundant vegetation. They enter their pupal stage for winter and emerge as adults in spring. Still others are able to acclimate themselves slowly to the cold and spend the winter as adults in protected environments. In fact, insects live through winter in all stages, but each species has a specific pattern which it always follows.

The next problem for the insect is when to emerge from diapause. This is slightly more complex, for many insects over-winter in total darkness and therefore cannot use light-dark ratios to time their emergence. Emergence is also complicated by the fact that their food sources — plants, other insects, or mammals — may not be ready in spring when warmth returns.

It has been theorized that in the heads of insects there are light receptors that, when exposed to the light-dark ratios of fall, produce a chemical. This chemical induces preparation behavior and diapause. During winter it gradually breaks down, possibly aided by the cold. When the chemical has finally disintegrated, the insect resumes its normal body processes and emerges. Each species would produce its own amount of the chemical in order to time its emergence to coincide with optimal life and food conditions.

These theories have been proven for only a minute percentage of all insects and are therefore quite speculative, yet the general principles of light-dark ratio as the starter of the winter clock and the chemical breakdown as the timing have been shown to operate also in other animals and plants. This would lead us to believe that these are general occurrences functioning in many life forms.

Chart of Evidence of Insects

GALLERIES AND CARVINGS IN WOOD

Bark Beetles
Carpenter Ants

GALLS ON PLANTS

on Blueberry — Blueberry Stem Gall
on Goldenrod — Elliptical Goldenrod Gall
Goldenrod Ball Gall
Goldenrod Bunch Gall
on Oak — Oak Apple Gall
Oak Bullet Gall
Oak Twig Gall
on Spruce — Spruce Pineapple Gall
on Willow — Willow Petaled Gall
Willow Pine Cone Gall

ACTIVE WINTER INSECTS

Springtails
Stoneflies

WASP NESTS

Paper Wasp nest

Hornet nest
Mud Dauber nest

WEB NESTS IN TREES

Eastern Tent Caterpillar
Fall Webworm

Natural History Descriptions

Bark Beetles (Family *Scolytidae*)

Bark Beetles are small, inconspicuous insects that spend most of their lives under the surface of tree bark. They seem an unlikely candidate for a book on the common natural sights of winter, but the reason for their inclusion is the prominence of the adult and larval tunnels that appear like engravings on the surface wood of dead trees. Many of these engravings form delightful patterns that record the fascinating life habits of the beetles.

Bark Beetles can be either monogamous, bigamous, or polygamous. Among the monogamous beetles, the female starts the egg tunnels herself after mating, being sometimes later helped by the male. Among bigamous or polygamous beetles, the male first bores through the bark and creates an enlarged cavity, called a *nuptial chamber*. Two or more females will enter this chamber, mate with the male, and dig their egg tunnels leading off from the chamber.

After this, the beetles' life histories are similar. The female digs an egg tunnel in the wood surface, depositing eggs in small niches at either side. The larvae hatch and eat their own tunnels through the wood; each of these "larval mines" increases in size as the larva grows. When finished with eating, each hollows out a chamber, where it pupates

Bark Beetle

(forms a cocoon) and transforms into an adult. As adults, the beetles emerge through the bark and fly to new host trees.

Bark Beetles winter over as larvae, pupae, or adults. Peeling away the bark of an infested tree will reveal them, but chances of seeing the insect are slight, since it is only about ⅒ inch long. And when the beetles are in a tree it is hard to guess at their presence. Even so, they have many predators, chiefly Woodpeckers, which feast on the beetles all year and especially in winter.

The Bark Beetle family, *Scolytidae*, is divided into three groups, distinguished by their habits: True Bark Beetles bore between the bark and the wood, Wood-eating Beetles bore into the wood, and Ambrosia Beetles bore into the wood and live off fungi that grow in their galleries.

Only True Bark Beetles are included here, for their galleries are most evident. There are many genera, some of the more important being *Scolytus, Dendroctonus,* and *Ips.* No genus is consistently represented by one type of egg tunnel, so that to label each type with only one or two genera would be misleading. I have therefore left the generic names out and stressed the construction of the tunnels and what they reveal about their makers. However, each species builds its tunnels in only certain types of trees, and often consistently on a certain part of that tree — for example, the lower branches, the upper branches, or the trunk. With continued observation you will soon be able to guess where certain patterns are likely to be found.

SIMPLE EGG TUNNELS

These tunnels are formed by a single monogamous female. They may be bored with, across, or regardless of the grain, depending on the species. They may be winding or straight, 1 inch to more than 1 foot long. There are almost always

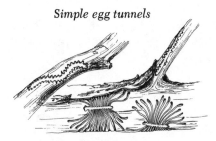

Simple egg tunnels

egg niches carved in their sides. Larval mines, radiating from the tunnels, may show in the wood or may have been bored in the bark and thus may not show on the wood surface.

FORKED EGG TUNNELS

These tunnels are made by either monogamous or bigamous beetles. They have an extended entrance tunnel that forks

Forked egg tunnels

off in opposite directions or in the same direction. They most commonly go across the grain of branches. Sometimes larval mines and even egg niches are bored in the bark and do not show on the wood surface.

RADIATE EGG TUNNELS

These are formed exclusively by polygamous beetles. The egg tunnels may be in a star pattern, either with the grain or

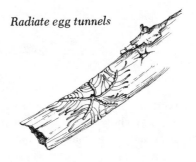

Radiate egg tunnels

across it. Sometimes the nuptial chamber is bored in the bark and does not show in the wood surface.

CAVE EGG TUNNELS

These tunnels are considered the most primitive form; they are made by either monogamous or polygamous beetles.

Cave egg tunnels

They are enlarged cavities in which all the eggs are laid in a group. The larvae eat together around the walls of the chamber, making it a large irregular shape.

IRREGULAR EGG TUNNELS

This category is given just to admit that Bark Beetle behavior is not as neat and simple as the first four examples would

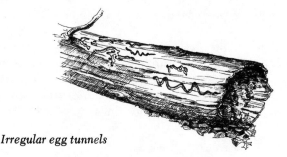

Irregular egg tunnels

suggest. Many of the Bark Beetles' tunnels are crisscrossing mazes with varying amounts of regularity.

Carpenter Ants (*Camponotus* species)

Evidence of Carpenter Ants as well as the ants themselves are frequent sights in winter. Often, in standing dead trees, you will find the carved galleries of these ants. They excavate into the dry wood of dead trees, and some species even burrow into living wood. Alive or dead, the wood must be in contact with the ground in order to allow for tunneling in both dry and moist conditions. The tunnels are used to protect the colony and raise the young. Both moist and dry areas are needed in order to keep the eggs, larvae, and

Carpenter Ant galleries

pupae at the proper temperature and humidity for healthy growth.

Unlike termites, Carpenter Ants do not eat the wood of their tunnels, but they carefully carry each particle of sawdust and drop it outside the nest. In dry wood the nest takes on a smooth sculptured look, like an intricate latticework.

Like that of most ants, and similar to that of the social

*Carpenter Ant; female worker,
queen, and male drone*

wasps, a Carpenter Ant society is made up of a fertile queen, which in Carpenter Ants may live as long as 15 years, males, which are short-lived and die after fertilization, and infertile females, which are the workers and soldiers. The workers are sometimes divided into two divisions, major and minor, depending on their size. The main job of the colony is to reproduce itself, which necessitates excavating the nest, rearing and protecting the young, and establishing new colonies. As winter approaches, egg laying ceases and the young are brought to maturity. The colony heads for the center of a log or to the underground part of their nest in order to minimize the rigors of winter. Here they hibernate in clusters and are often found in logs that have been split for firewood. They become active at anytime in winter when the temperature rises well above freezing.

An enemy of Carpenter Ants' in winter is the Pileated Woodpecker, which pecks huge holes in trees in order to feed on the ants. Often the empty galleries of Carpenter Ants are reused by other genera of ants as well as by other insects. The openings in the wood also enable moisture and fungi, which help speed the process of decay, to enter.

GALLS

Galls are deformations of plants caused by insects and used by them for food and protection while developing. There are over 1,500 insects in North America that cause gall formations. Most likely everyone has seen galls, but few may have recognized them as such. Many are evident in summer as swellings, growths, or discolorations on the leaves of trees and plants; still others are more clearly seen in winter as deformations of twigs.

Galls have received scientific attention for three main reasons: they often interfere with agricultural productivity, particularly that of wheat; believed to be examples of tumorous growth, they are studied from the viewpoint of cancer research; and the life histories of the gall-makers are often unusual and intriguingly complex.

But even with this interest and study, the process of gall formation is still unclear and the life histories of the majority of gall-makers remain a mystery. The closest we can come to explaining gall formation is to say that the insect disrupts the normal growth of a plant either through physical irritation or chemical secretion. Around the insect, the plant grows a deformity, which the insect then uses for food and protection while developing.

Some galls have just one maker, others harbor many individuals. A number of insects use galls made by others. Those that do not hurt the gall-maker are called *inquilines*; those that kill the gall-maker are parasites. Even after a gall is left by its maker it is used as shelter by many other insects, especially in winter. These galls are in turn opened by birds and mammals seeking the insects inside. As you look for the galls included here you will certainly find many others, and will begin to realize what a common phenomenon gall formation is.

Blueberry Stem Gall

The advantage of knowing this gall is that it enables you to identify Highbush Blueberry, one of the most common shrubs in the winter woods. In many books this gall is called Huckleberry Stem Gall, but it is most common on Blueberry bushes. A gall wasp, or Cynipid (*Hemadas nubilipennis*), causes it to grow.

The gall starts forming in early summer and is initiated in the cambium, the active growing layer, of young twigs. Its growth deforms the twig by making it bend downward. By fall, the gall is red-brown and kidney-shaped. In spring it will become riddled with holes bored by emerging adult wasps, showing that the gall is polythalamous — containing more than one chamber. Some flies are also known to inhabit this gall as inquilines.

Blueberry Stem Galls:
left is young, right is old.

In winter you may find both this year's and last year's galls, the former brown and smooth, the latter gray, riddled with holes, and farther back on the twig.

Elliptical Goldenrod Gall

This is one of the most widespread and common galls found in winter. It is formed by the larva of a moth (*Gnorimo-*

Goldenrod with Elliptical Gall

schema gallaesolidaginis), an unusual situation, for very few moths cause galls. In fall the adult moth lays its eggs singly on the lower leaves and stems of Goldenrod. The egg develops to a prehatching state in fall and overwinters in that stage. In spring the larva hatches, crawls toward new Goldenrod shoots, burrows into the end buds, and travels down inside the stem. When it has gone a few inches down, it stops and continues to feed in that place. At this point the plant begins to form the gall around the insect. The larva continues to feed until late July, then bores an exit hole in the upper end of the gall, so that when it is a nonboring adult it will be able to emerge. Before pupating, it plugs up the hole with a mixture of silk and plant material. It then pupates, emerging later in August and September as an adult.

Elliptical Goldenrod Gall

Thus, the normal Elliptical Goldenrod Gall will not contain its maker in winter — it will have an open exit hole at its top and a shed red-brown pupal skin arranged inside with the head up. But there are many parasites of this moth and you will often find evidence of their work in the winter galls. A common parasite is the Ichneumon wasp, *Calliephialtes notandus*. The Ichneumon wasp has a long ovipositor (egg despositor), which it can insert into the gall in order to lay an egg on the larva. The intruding insect eats the larva, spins a long thin brown cocoon in which to pupate, and emerges as an adult in late summer.

Another wasp, known as *Copidosoma gelechiae*, deposits

Interior of Elliptical Goldenrod Gall. From left to right: shiny brown pupal skin of original maker, then white cocoon and brown cocoon of parasites

its egg in the egg of the moth that makes the Elliptical Goldenrod Gall. The moth larva develops normally until pupation, then dies. The larva of the parasite hatches, develops, and pupates in the moth larva. The wasps emerge in late summer. Evidence of their work is a larval skin riddled with holes, lying inside the winter gall. There are others that overwinter in the gall as adults or pupae, either in a brown and white cocoon or naked in the gall.

Besides these parasites there are numerous Arthropods that reuse the empty galls. In particular, many spiders use them for shelter or for a protected spot in which to place their egg cases. Also reported present in empty Elliptical Goldenrod Galls are bees, ants, beetles, and thrips.

Goldenrod Ball Gall

The Goldenrod Ball Gall is an abrupt round swelling on the plant stem. It is common; sometimes it will be present on most of the Goldenrod of a given field, occasionally with more than one on a single stem.

Goldenrod Ball Gall

The gall is caused by the larva of a small spotted-winged fly (*Eurosta solidaginis*). After mating, the female fly lays its eggs on the new stems in late May and June. The egg hatches, and the larva burrows into the stem. Here it continues to hollow out a chamber slightly larger than its body size, while the plant forms the gall around it. It is mature by the onset of winter and overwinters in the larval form. In spring the larva resumes activity by eating a tunnel just as far as the outside layer of the gall. It then reenters its chamber, where it pupates. The adult fly crawls out the hole and bursts through the outer skin of the gall.

Thus, normally the Goldenrod Ball Gall contains its maker in winter. But there are many other insects that regularly take advantage of the helpless larvae. In this case small beetles often enter the galls and eat the larvae before hibernating in the galls themselves.

Goldenrod Bunch Gall

This is another of the more common and easily recognizable Goldenrod galls. It is formed by a midge, *Rhopalomyia*

Goldenrod Bunch Gall

solidaginis, and is reportedly found only on Canada Goldenrod (*Solidago canadensis*). Initiated in the leaf bud, it creates a stunting of stem growth along with a proliferation of leaves, so that the final gall appears like a flower with many woody petals. Occurring always at the tip of the winter stalk, it is easily spotted in a grove of Goldenrod plants.

Each Bunch Gall appears to be caused by a single larva, since there is generally one cavity at the center of the gall;

some other midges from the same genus are known to be inquilines. The specific name for the gall-maker, as with those of the other Goldenrod galls mentioned, is derived from the generic name for Goldenrod, *Solidago*.

Oak Galls

Oaks host more types of gall-makers than any other plant. Of the nearly 1,500 North American galls so far discovered, over 800 have been found on Oaks. Galls seem to form on all parts of Oaks: the roots, trunk, branches, and twigs, leaves, flowers, and fruit (acorns). By far the greatest number form on the leaves, the next largest on the twigs. Once you become aware of these galls you can often recognize Oaks in winter just by noticing the number of deformities on the branches.

Almost all Oak galls are formed by a family of wasps called *Cynipidae* or Cynipids, or sometimes gall-wasps, because so many members utilize galls in different stages of their development. Many of these wasps are known to have alternating generations — one generation without males, the other with both sexes. But the life histories of the majority of these Cynipids, even the most common, still remain completely unknown. Study of them is made difficult by the fact that the generations of a single insect may form different galls, even on different host plants.

Below are shown three of the most common types of galls seen on Oaks in winter. For simplification of identification, many books on insects state that certain species are responsible for each of these types. But this oversimplification hides the astounding diversity of the galls and their subtle differences, for each of these three types of gall has many variations, each made by a different species of insect.

Oak Apple Galls

Oak Apple Galls appear as small tan balls, between 1 and 2 inches in diameter. They are formed on the leaves, frequently on the leaf mid-vein or the leaf stem (petiole), and often initiated in the leaf bud itself. There are two groups: the ones that form in spring on the growing leaf, and the ones that form on the matured leaf in late summer and fall. The spring ones tend to be soft; the late-summer galls tend to have harder shells and to develop more slowly. Obviously the late-summer galls will be more common in winter. You may find them on the ground or hanging on the tree like Christmas ornaments. Sometimes a small sapling will be covered with twenty to thirty galls, looking quite festive in the winter woods.

These galls are divided into two categories depending on their internal structure: full and empty. Full Oak Apples

*Oak Apple Galls: one pecked open by a bird,
the other split in half to show interior*

contain spongy growth between their hard center chambers and their outer shells, whereas the empty Oak Apples have just minute radiating fibers connecting the chambers with the shells.

As is the case with other galls, Oak Apples may contain many inquilines, parasites, or reusers. Opening up galls can be enjoyable, for you are never quite sure what you are going to find. In summer I once opened an Oak Apple, only to find a group of over a hundred eggs, with as many ants, who streamed onto my fingers from inside the gall. Another time I found mud nests of wasps inside.

Amphibolops and *Cynips* are two of the more common genera of insects that cause Oak Apple Galls. There are at least one hundred different types of Oak Apples, varying in size, shape, surface texture, and the part of the leaf on which they form.

Oak Bullet Galls

As their name suggests, these are small hard round galls about the size of marbles. Unlike the Oak Apples, which grow on leaf parts, these are produced only on twigs. They

Oak Bullet Galls

can be found singly, in groups of two or three, or in clusters of twenty or more depending on the specific type of Bullet Gall. So far there have been over fifty types of Bullet Galls discovered in North America, the most common gall wasps forming them being members of the genus *Disholcapsis*.

Twig and Branch Galls

This is a very general category, included here because its varied members are so commonly seen in winter. Oak Bullet Galls are actually also in this category, but have been mentioned separately because of their distinct shape. The other

Oak twig and branch galls

members included here tend to be irregular swellings and deformities growing at the ends of Oak twigs. Unlike both the Bullet and Oak Apple galls, each gall contains many larvae.

They have been given such common names as Oak Potato Galls, Gouty Oak Galls, and Oak Club Galls. Members of the genera *Neuroterus* and *Plagiotrochus* are among the most common causes of these galls.

Spruce Pineapple Gall

Spruce Pineapple Galls form at the tips of Spruce branches where new growth is occurring and remain on the tree until the branch is shed. They look like miniature pineapples, between ½ and 1 inch long; often spines of old needles protrude from them.

The gall insect (*Chermes abietis*) belongs to the aphid

Spruce Pineapple Gall

Spruce tree with galls

family, a group that tends to have extremely complex life cycles involving what is called "alternation of generations." Parent A lays eggs, which develop into parent B. Parent B lays eggs, which in turn develop into a new parent A. The two generations may resemble each other or may be totally different in appearance. Therefore, it is often difficult to trace the life histories of aphids. Some other aphids are even more difficult to follow since they may have as many as five distinct generations before a return to parent A.

The Spruce Gall maker has only two generations, which complete their cycle in a single year. But, as if to offset this simplicity, *Chermes abietis* has no males in its species; all reproduction is parthenogenetic (partheno=virgin, genetic =birth). The cycle starts in fall with a winged female, parent A, which flies to a Spruce and lays eggs at the base of the needle buds. These eggs hatch into wingless female nymphs, parent B, which eat the Spruce needles in fall and overwinter at the base of the spring needle buds. In spring they resume feeding, and the needles swell and grow together, forming the gall. Soon the nymphs lay eggs, which hatch, feed on the needles, enter the gall, and emerge as winged females. These are parents A, which fly to new Spruces and start the cycle over. Thus the galls are not occupied in winter, but are used in spring by generation A.

Willow Petaled Gall

One of the most beautiful winter galls, the Willow Petaled Gall, looks like a gray flower at the tip of a Willow shrub. These galls are often numerous, frequently seen on the same plant as the lovely Willow Pine Cone Gall. The Willow Petaled Gall is believed to be caused by the gall midge *Rhabdophaga rhodoides;* it starts forming in late spring and early summer when the plant is actively growing. Little is known of the gall's life history, except that the loose petals undoubtedly harbor many hibernating insects during winter.

Willow Petaled Gall, both whole and split open

This gall, along with the Willow Pine Cone Gall and Goldenrod Bunch Gall, is believed by some to be composed of modified leaves bunched together with no stem elongation in between. Cutting these three types of gall in half reveals their similar internal structure.

Willow Pine Cone Gall

This gall appears only on Willow shrubs and is more common in the Great Lakes area than in the East. One of the most beautiful, it is shaped like a small, tightly closed pine cone and forms only at the tips of branches. A small gnat, or midge (*Rhabdophaga strobiloides*), just two tenths of an inch long is its maker. The family this insect belongs to, *Cecidomyiae*, contains many other gall-producing gnats.

The gnat's life cycle is refreshingly simple for a gallmaker. During winter it is a larva in the center of the gall.

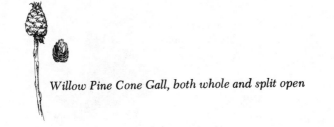

Willow Pine Cone Gall, both whole and split open

In spring it pupates and emerges as an adult. The fertilized female then lays eggs on the new growth at the Willow branch tips. The larvae hatch, stimulate gall growth, and spend the winter in the gall.

What has attracted attention to this gall, besides its beauty, is the tremendous number of other insects that use it for overwintering and breeding, some as inquilines, others as parasites. For one study 23 galls were collected and 564 insects were reared from them. Only 15 contained the original host gnat, but in addition there were 6 wasp parasites, 169 other guest gnats, and 384 eggs of the Meadow Grasshopper (*Xiphidium eusiferum*). Clearly, the overlapping scales of this gall have proved to be extremely valuable to other insects that have adapted to taking advantage of this gnat's gall-causing ability.

ACTIVE WINTER INSECTS

Springtail (*Achorutes nivicolus*)

If you continue to explore nature in winter you are bound to come across "Snow Fleas." At the base of a tree on warmer winter days or where the sun has melted through to a patch of leaves, you may see the surrounding snow darkened with small black dots. It may at first appear to be soot on the surface of the snow, but as you look closer you will see

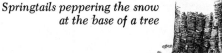

Springtails peppering the snow at the base of a tree

thousands of tiny gray insects hopping about. These are the "snow fleas," which are actually called Springtails, or *Achorutes nivicolus.*

They belong to a primitive but widely distributed order of wingless insects called *Collembola.* Members of this order generally inhabit the surface of the soil, but they also live on the surface of ponds and in tidal zones. They inhabit both temperate and tropical climates and are most often vegetarians, feeding on algae, pollen, and leaf mold. They are so prevalent that they often number well over ten million individuals per acre.

Their common name, Springtail, refers to the two ap-

Springtails

pendages they have on their last body segment. These are like two modified legs, which are normally folded against their abdomen and held in place by two clasps. When the clasps open, these two appendages spring against the ground, propelling the insect a few inches away. This flea-like leaping motion has given them the misleading name, "snow fleas."

Species *Achorutes nivicolus* comes out to feed in winter, taking advantage of microclimates in the sun that may be much warmer than air temperatures. Once you spot them you will begin to notice them more and more, for although they are inconspicuous at first, they are quite common.

Stonefly (Order *Plecoptera*)

The Stonefly is another insect that is often active in winter. In fact some species of stoneflies have adjusted their cycle to

Stoneflies crawling on rocks

the exact opposite of those of most other insects. Their larvae, which live in streams, start feeding and growing in fall and early winter. The adults emerge from the water in midwinter and mate on the shores; then the female lays her eggs back in the water.

When they fly slowly through the air they appear like

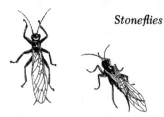

Stoneflies

large gray mosquitoes. But they are more often found crawling over rocks and snow at stream edges, where as adults they come to feed on algae. These insects live in only clean rushing water, the larvae living and feeding under stones at the river's edge.

WASPS

Paper Wasp (*Polistes fuscatus*)

The nest of this wasp is just a single layer of comb made with paper, with as few as 10 to as many as 150 cells. This layer is usually placed under the eaves of buildings or sheds or under large branches. It is hung with the cell openings

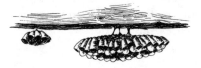

Paper Wasp nests: one aborted, one completed

facing downward and is attached by usually a single thread-like pedicel (stalk).

You need a simplified life history of these wasps in order to interpret all that you might see in relation to the nest. Male and female wasps mate in the fall, and both go into hibernation in rock crevices and rotting logs. Only the queens live through the winter, emerging in the first warm days of spring to fly around and seek out a good nesting site. Once one has been found, the queen starts building a few cells and lays an egg in each one. At this time, other queens, which for some reason did not complete their nests, join our queen and become subservient workers for her, finishing cells that she initiates and feeding the larvae when they hatch from the eggs. After the larvae are full-grown

Paper Wasp on nest

white grubs, they seal off their cells and pupate, emerging later as more female workers.

At the end of summer the queen lays more eggs, some that are fertilized and others that aren't. These eggs are fed extra amounts of food and develop into idle males and queens. These two types hang around the nest and are fed by the female workers. Soon the original queen stops laying eggs and the nest starts to break up. The workers stop working so hard; sometimes they eat the partially developed grubs. In fall the males and new queens leave the nest, mate, and hibernate. And the queens with extra reserves of fat stored in their bodies live through the winter to start the cycle over.

The nest itself reflects a great deal about the wasps' lives. It is made with dried wood and plant fibers, which are gathered from fenceposts, old buildings, and dead trees. Bits of wood are ripped off while held fast in the wasp's mandibles (mouth parts). They are taken to the nest, chewed, mixed with a saliva, and applied as paper pulp in circular additions to each cell. On some nests you can see the variation in color of these additions, reflecting the different sources of the wood.

The queen initiates the building of all cells with a small basal outline. The other workers complete them. You may find that some of the outer cells are half as long. These are queen-initiated but unfinished. You may also find a nest of just a few cells — this was started by a queen in spring but for some reason she left it and became a worker for another queen.

The single thread that attaches the nest to the limb or eave is believed to be a protective adaptation. With just one source of access by crawling parasites, the nest can be defended more easily, and in some species the queen coats this thread with a substance repellent to ants. The top of the cells are also usually coated with a shiny substance that makes the paper water-resistant.

The cells are built and filled concentrically, and when the first grubs are hatched, the initial cells are sometimes cleaned and used again. Some of the cells may have remains of larvae still in them; others may be sealed off and when opened found to contain dead but developed wasps. The lives of the workers are short, and there are rarely as many wasps as there are cells at any given time.

Often the nests are found on the ground in winter, blown there by the wind. Other good spots for seeing them are in abandoned sheds, garages, barns, and under the eaves of wooden buildings.

Hornets, Yellow Jackets (*Vespula* species)

The paper nests of Hornets and Yellow Jackets (*Vespulae*) are considered more advanced than the open nests of *Polistes*, for they afford more protection from enemies and harsh environmental conditions. Basically their life cycle is the same as that of *Polistes* except that only a single queen starts the hive and she is never joined by other queens. She makes a few cells attached to a branch, lays eggs in them, and proceeds to surround them with an envelope of paper. She then feeds the larva until they pupate and emerge as adult female workers. After that the workers do the food gathering, nest building, and brood tending, while the queen lays eggs. In fall the queen will lay eggs that will hatch into males or fertile females; the adult insects will mate, and the fertilized females will winter over, emerging in the spring to start new nests.

The nests are abandoned in winter and can be safely collected and inspected after below-freezing weather has definitely set in. They can be built at almost any level from 2 to 40 feet off the ground. They are often in trees or shrubs and sometimes under the eaves of house roofs. They also vary in size from 8 to 18 inches in depth, those of Yellow Jackets often being the smaller ones.

After the first workers hatch they start to build new cells and enlarge the nest, chewing away the inner layers of the

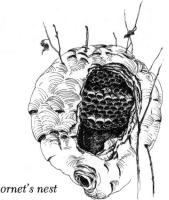

Cut-open Hornet's nest

envelope and adding new layers to the outside. Paper is made by collecting strips of dried wood, chewing them, and adding a fluid that acts like a glue to hold the paper together. If you examine the outside of the nest you can see the wood of different colors, added on in arcs that curve away from the hive. This makes the layers "quilted" and holds them apart so that their insulating affect is maximized. Most nests have between 6 and 8 layers of paper, the total covering averaging 2 inches in thickness.

It has been proven that Hornets can regulate the temperature of their nest. In one experiment it was shown that where outdoor temperatures varied as much as 40 degrees F. over a week, temperatures inside the hive varied only 5 degrees. Much of this consistency is due to temperature regulating by the wasps, but some of the evenness is certainly caused by this efficient insulation of the nest.

If you cut open part of the nest you are likely to see two to four tiers of egg cells arranged one beneath the other. Some of the outer cells may be short, which means they were never finished; some cells may contain dried larvae, which means the nest was abandoned before they matured. Other cells have an added white layer of paper. These cells were going to be used a second time. The first time, the larva excreted its feces in the bottom of the cell, and since this makes the cell too short for the next larva, the workers, instead of cleaning it out, just add an extension to the cell. If you poke into the bottom of these cells you will find the excrement packed there.

Yellow Jacket and Hornet

The entrance to the hive is a hole usually placed on one side of the base of the nest. Although the wasps abandon this nest in winter, it is still an excellent winter home, and many other types of insects and spiders spend the winter within it.

These same nests also are built underground by both Hornets and Yellow Jackets. Usually placed in a mammal burrow or natural cavity, they are often found in fall, ripped open by Skunks or Raccoons, who were seeking the grubs when the insects were slowed by the cold.

Mud Daubers (Family *Sphecidae*)

Mud Daubers are solitary rather than social; they have no caste system, just males and females. After mating, the females build nests, provision them with paralyzed insects, lay their eggs in them, and seal them off. The young larvae feed on the living but paralyzed flesh of the stored insects. The Mud Daubers overwinter in the stage of larval growth that just precedes pupation. In spring they pupate and emerge as adults.

Yellow Mud Dauber on nest

In the *Sphecidae* family there are two common wasps which build mud nests and a third which reuses these nests. The nests are built on bridges, house eaves, and in sheds, garages, and barns. The wasps prefer to build in places that are dry, warm, and well supplied with especially spiders.

The Yellow Mud Dauber, *Sceliphron caementarium,* collects mud on warm days from the edges of ponds, puddles, and streams. It first lays down a mud foundation on its building surface, then adds half-arcs of mud, alternating from right to left to form a chamber. About thirty trips to collect mud are needed to make one cell, and each cell takes one to two hours of constant building to complete. After the cell is packed with paralyzed spiders and a single egg, the wasp seals it off with a mud cap. More cells are added to this one, and all of them may then be covered over with a layer of mud.

Old nests often persist for a year or two and another wasp, the Blue Mud Dauber, *Chalybion californicum,* cleans and repairs these nests for its own use. It carries water in its crop to the old nest. With this it dissolves old mud in order to make repairs and seal off the cells. The reuse of nests obviously saves time, allowing the wasp to do more food collecting and egg laying, with the result that these wasps are often more numerous than the species that originally made the nest.

A second group of nest builders are in the genus *Trypoxylon,* a few species of which build long separate tubes. The shape of their nests has led to their being called Pipe-Organ

Wasps. Unlike those of the Yellow Mud Dauber, their nests are not covered over with an extra mud layer, and each tube consists of many cells. Each of these cells contains spiders and an egg and is separated from the others with mud dividers.

Sometimes you can carefully remove mud nests intact and scrap away a portion of the mud backing to reveal what is inside. Depending on the time of year and the condition of the cell, you may find spiders and a larva, a dormant larva, a pupa, or an empty cocoon.

WEB BUILDERS

The two moths described below, though belonging to separate families, are related in habits through their use of protective web nests during their larval stage. The nests are not particularly attractive in winter, when they appear as ragged masses of webbing filled with dried leaves and crumbling excrement, but they are so common a sight with the leaves gone that they bear some attention. Also, from a distance they can fool you into thinking they are birds' nests, and you should be able to tell the difference.

Since these insects are most conspicuous when they are larvae, both have been named for the larval stage: Tent Caterpillar and Fall Webworm.

Eastern Tent Caterpillar (*Malacosoma americana*)

One type of webby mass hanging from trees belongs to the Tent Caterpillars. Their webs are built primarily in the crotches of branches and serve a very different purpose from those of the Fall Webworm. In spring, when the eggs first hatch, the caterpillars crawl down the branch to the first large joining of two branches. Here they build a web

Old nest of Tent Caterpillar

for protection from such predators as birds and other insects. In order to feed, they leave the nest and crawl up the branches to the leaves.

The webbed nest is made communally and soon becomes filled with the remains of the caterpillar feces, as well as molted skins, for the larva, like insects in all stages of growth, must shed its skin as it grows. The caterpillars continue to add on layers of webbing, so that the final nest is

Moth and larva of Tent Caterpillar

made of many layers filled with excrement and molted skins. This stage lasts six weeks. At this point, after a certain number of molts or instars (periods between molting), they drop from the nest and spin cocoons in sheltered areas, leaving their former gregarious mode of life.

In three weeks they emerge as adult moths, then they soon mate and the females lay their egg masses on host twigs. These egg masses can also be found in winter. They

Egg mass of Tent Caterpillar

contain 100 to 300 eggs and are surrounded with a shiny, waterproof, foamy material. A group of Black Cherry or Chokecherry trees with webs hanging from them is an excellent place to spot the egg cases.

Fall Webworm (*Hyphantria cunea*)

The Fall Webworm, like the Tent Caterpillar, builds a communal nest of webbing. But it is built in late summer and is more likely to last into fall and winter. The nests differ in location from those of Tent Caterpillars, reflecting their different use. Fall Webworms start to build their nest at the branch tips and enclose leaves with the webbing. As the leaves are enclosed the caterpillars eat them and extend

Old nests of Fall Webworm

the nest over new leaves as they are needed. Thus the finished product is not a triangular web in the crotch of branches, but a long loose web that encases the end of a twig. In winter these can mislead one into thinking they are the nest of the Baltimore Oriole, which is a similar color and hangs from branch tips. But an Oriole nest contains no leaves and is spherical at the base.

Another interesting contrast with the Tent Caterpillar is the life history of the Fall Webworm. Its eggs hatch in summer rather than spring, often being attached to the

Moth and larva of Fall Webworm

underside of leaves of host plants. The larvae feed, never leaving their nest. As fall approaches they leave the web and head for bark crevices and leaf litter. Here they weave cocoons and stay in the pupal form throughout winter, in striking contrast to the long period the Tent Caterpillars spend as eggs. In May the adult Webworm moths emerge from the pupa, mate, and lay eggs.

The webs, like the Tent Caterpillars', are similarly filled with excrement and molted skins, but in addition contain skeletonized leaves.

V

Winter's Birds
and Abandoned Nests

*E*VER SINCE THE MELTING of the last glacier that covered much of North America, animals and plants have been slowly advancing to the North to claim unutilized habitats. Most birds can live comfortably in the North during summer, but in winter only a relatively few species are sufficiently adapted to survive. Probably the most important factor influencing which birds can remain North and which birds must return South, is a bird's ability to acquire food.

Two major aspects of winter substantially alter the availability of food; they are the cold and the snow. Cold most affects the food sources of water birds. It causes much of the water plant life to die back and makes many water animals recede into the mud to hibernate. The cold also freezes over lakes and streams, making what food still exists inaccessible. This lack causes inland water birds such as Herons, Ducks, Rails, and Sandpipers either to fly south to open water or to live by the sea, where more food is available.

Cold also affects another important source of food — airborne insects. Many birds depend solely on catching insects in the air and are specifically adapted to doing so. Insects cannot withstand the cold and are generally dormant throughout winter. Birds such as Flycatchers, Swifts, and Warblers must fly south in order to find aerial insects.

Snow, the other factor of winter that limits food sources, restricts those ground-feeding birds that eat insects or small animals — birds such as Robins, Thrashers, and Towhees. Snow also hides the movements of small rodents in fields, making it harder for some Hawks and Owls to catch their prey. These birds must move south to where snow cover is at most intermittent.

Birds that stay north in winter or come south from the arctic tundra are the ones that can live off the available food sources. Two sources are primary in winter: insects and seeds.

Hibernating insects are especially available on trees, where they overwinter in bark crevices, on buds, within the wood, or on needles, and about half of our small winter birds live off them. You will always find these birds in woodlands, often in mixed flocks, flitting among trees, searching above or beneath trunks and limbs for insect eggs, larvae, pupae, or adults. These birds include the Chickadees, Creepers, Titmice, Kinglets, Woodpeckers, and Nuthatches.

The other main source of winter food is the marvelously abundant fall harvest of tree and weed seeds and shrub berries. Almost half of all our winter birds use these as their primary source of food in winter. The number of plants that provide food of this kind are too numerous to begin to name; coniferous trees are particularly important, as of course are hedgerow shrubs and winter weeds. Birds that utilize this winter food include the Finches, Sparrows, Mockingbirds, and Grosbeaks, as well as Chickadees and Nuthatches.

The third main source of winter food is available to scavengers: birds such as Crows, Pigeons, and Gulls, which are not particular about what they eat and are not overly specialized in their feeding habits. These birds live off human refuse through most of the winter, frequenting dumps and city parks, using street litter and road kills. They are not shy of humans and seem to live and prosper on what we throw away.

Popular interest in birds during the last fifty years has centered on identification; amassing a "life list," which puts the emphasis on new species and encourages neglect of and disdain for the most common. This approach poses a problem for both the beginning and advanced bird-watcher in winter, for there are only twenty to thirty land bird species commonly present in winter, and they are already known by the experienced and easily learned by the beginner. So, after you know the name of a bird, what next? This is a serious and difficult question, and within its answer lie our deepest beliefs on the value of nature to humans. The question must be continually asked in order to avoid the empty naming of objects in nature.

One suggestion of an avenue of further involvement with birds is to take the time to observe their behavior — the relationship of birds to their environment and to other birds. And actually, winter is a particularly good time in which to do this, for with leaves gone, birds are more easily seen, and many join together in flocks, making them even more conspicuous. Now is the time to take birds you may have dismissed all summer as "just a Mockingbird" or "only another Chickadee" and relate to them on a deeper level of interest.

There are four areas of bird behavior to look for in winter: feeding, territorial, social, and breeding.

Eating enough food to keep warm is the main activity of birds in winter. The quantity and distribution of a bird's food determine most of its daily movements. Knowing what, how, when, and where a bird eats quickly involves you with the bird's physical structure and relationship to its environment. A bird's feet, bill, and feathers are primarilly adapted to feeding. How and in what way for each bird? Stop and watch birds feed in the wild; begin to learn the plants birds feed on, which are most favored and therefore lose their berries or seeds first, which ones aren't eaten all winter. Observe the variety of ways birds utilize food. A Cardinal may eat a Red Cedar berry whole, but a Chickadee will hold it in its feet, peck out the seeds, and let the fleshy part fall. Nuthatches can open nuts, often wedging them in tree bark and then battering them. Woodpeckers will peck into Oak Apple Galls to get insects that are inside. Nothing ties together a knowledge of nature as well as observing feeding habits, for they underlie and structure the larger parts of animal life.

Territorial behavior is also easily observed in winter, for two of our most common birds establish and maintain clearly defined winter territories. The Mockingbird, with a variety of displays and calls, establishes a territory in late fall which contains adequate food for the winter. When more than one Mockingbird settles on an area in fall, the displays are easily seen and the stages of territorial development are exciting to follow from week to week. Chickadees also establish territory in winter, each area lived in by a flock rather than by individual birds. Through observation in winter, you can estimate the extent of their territories and locate their favorite feeding areas.

Territory is generally defined as an area defended against intruders. But many other winter birds live in well-defined areas they do not defend. These areas are called ranges. Titmice and Juncos as flocks, and Woodpeckers and Nuthatches as pairs or single birds, all inhabit defined ranges. Once you begin to notice one of these birds in a particular area, you can expect to see it there all winter, and the Woodpecker and Nuthatch may also remain there through the summer to breed.

The social behavior of birds is in some ways more easily observed in winter than summer since many birds gather into flocks for the winter. Social behavior within species includes the huge roosts of Starlings and Crows; the feeding behavior of Crows, with their sentinel posted; the coveys of Bobwhites, which roost in circular formations, and the order of dominance within Chickadee flocks. Social behavior also occurs between species, especially in the common mixed flocks of Titmice, Kinglets, Chickadees, and Woodpeckers, usually led by the Titmice or Chickadees. Mockingbirds and Jays interact with other birds that might compete for their winter food, and Crows mob Hawks and Owls whenever they spot them.

Most people believe that all things associated with breeding behavior happen in spring, but this is far from the case. The breeding of most mammals and the courtship of many birds occurs in the middle of winter. Particularly obvious and easily observed are the displays of Mallard and Black Ducks. The ducks are common in small park ponds and can be watched from close by. They have a large vocabulary of gestures which, once learned, are not hard to spot. The ducks display in varying amounts all winter, hitting their peak of activity in November and December. Hairy Woodpeckers also begin courtship displays in December, and their "drumming" on resonant trees starts to be heard at that time. Jays gather in early spring to engage in a strange group display during February and March.

All of these types of bird behavior can be enjoyed even by the beginner; there is no need to learn the names of all the birds before you begin to be involved. Relatively little is known about the winter behavior of many of our birds, however. Where studies have been made, I have selected the most observable aspects and included them in the natural history descriptions. For readers who want more detail, they should seek out the journals listed in the Bibliography.

Key to Winter's Birds

LARGE BIRDS (OVER 12 INCHES LONG), THE SIZE OF A CROW OR GULL

GULL, SPECIES — Large whitish bird with gray or black wings; frequently soars over coast, rivers, lakes, and dumps; immature birds are mottled brown and white. Illustrated: Herring Gull.

DUCK, SPECIES — Large flattened bill; large heavy body; webbed feet; often swimming in water. Illustrated: male Mallard.

CROW, COMMON — Large all-black bird; often in small, wary groups; frequently feeds on ground.

HAWK, SPECIES — Large or medium-sized bird; generally brownish in color; usually soaring overhead; sharp pointed down-curved bill. Illustrated: Rough-legged Hawk.

OWL, SPECIES — Heavyset bird, large or medium-sized; large circular patterns around eyes; large rounded head; generally roosts in trees during day; often chased by crows. Illustrated: Great Horned Owl.

PHEASANT, RING-NECKED — Good-sized, ground-feeding bird; long pointed tail, which trails behind when bird is in flight; generally brown, but male has white neck-ring and dark head with red surrounding eye. Illustrated: male.

GROUSE, RUFFED — Large, brownish, ground-feeding bird with fan-shaped tail; head feathers often ruffled into a crest; tail brown with black terminal band.

GROUSE, SPRUCE — Similar to Ruffed Grouse, but extremely tame; has black tail with brown terminal band; male is black on chin and breast. Illustrated: Ruffed Grouse.

MEDIUM-SIZED BIRDS (12–16 INCHES LONG), SIZE OF A ROBIN OR PIGEON

BOBWHITE — Medium-sized, brownish ground-feeding bird; black stripe through eye; short stubby tail.

LARK, HORNED — Black bib; black vertical stripe on light cheek; feeds on ground in open, barren areas; usually in flocks.

STARLING — Black medium-sized birds, speckled with white on breast and back; long, thin, pointed bill; by spring, speckles wear off and dark winter bill turns yellow.

GROSBEAK, EVENING — Black wing on yellowish bird; large whitish conical bill; patch of white on top of black wing; feeds in flocks, eating large seeds from trees; male has yellow forehead. Illustrated: male.

CARDINAL — Medium-sized bird with crest; male all red, female olive; both have reddish conical bill; frequently give a loud "chip . . . chip" call when disturbed.

JAY, BLUE — Medium-sized crested bird; bluish with white and black markings on wings; black bib from crest to around neck; in small, loose groups; often raucous.

JAY, GRAY — Medium-sized bird with a black patch on back of neck; no crest; common only in Canada and northern states. Illustrated: Blue Jay.

MOCKINGBIRD — Sleek, gray bird with long tail; light-colored underneath; shows large, obvious white patches on wings when flying; frequently gives a "chewk" call when disturbed.

DOVE, ROCK — Common street Pigeon; colored with shades of gray and iridescent green; when they take off, the sound of their wing tips hitting together can be heard.

DOVE, MOURNING — Buff-colored; similar to Pigeon but sleeker and with long pointed tail, particularly noticeable in flight; makes a whistling sound when taking off; generally in flocks.

GROSBEAK, PINE — Dark wing with white wing bars; short, heavy black bill; male reddish, female olive-green.

WOODPECKER, HAIRY — Climbs up tree trunks; black and white patterned; white stripe down back; bill is almost as long as depth of head; male has red patch on back of head. Illustrated: Hairy Woodpecker.

SMALL BIRDS (LESS THAN 6 INCHES LONG), SIZE OF A SPARROW

WOODPECKER, DOWNY — Same as Hairy Woodpecker, but smaller; bill only half as long as depth of head.

NUTHATCH, WHITE-BREASTED — Climbs up *and* down tree trunks; dark cap and black; white underneath; white face setting off dark eye.

CREEPER, BROWN — Climbs only up tree trunks; small; brown streaked on top, white underneath; long, thin, down-curved bill; seen singly in mixed flocks.

TITMOUSE, TUFTED — The only small, crested bird in winter; gray back, lighter underparts; often in mixed flocks in woodlands.

JUNCO, DARK-EYED — Dark gray bird with lighter underparts; light, pinkish bill; when Junco is in flight, sidetail feathers show two bands of white.

CHICKADEE, BLACK-CAPPED — A black-capped, black-chinned bird with white on cheek; small; often hangs upside down when feeding; tame and in flocks.

KINGLET, GOLDEN-CROWNED — Smallest bird of winter woods; olive- to brown-colored body with thin white wing bars; broad yellow stripe on top of head; short, thin bill.

GOLDFINCH, AMERICAN — Dark black wing on olive- to yellow-colored bird; small; thin white wing bars; short, light-colored bill; always gives a slight twittering call as it flies.

SISKIN, PINE — Heavily streaked, sleek, brown bird; patches of yellow on wings and tail (displayed best in flight); thin pointed bill; sometimes flock with Goldfinches.

FINCH, PURPLE — Female is brown-streaked; told from Sparrows by short, heavy, conical bill; male is reddish on head, back, and rump. Illustrated: female.

REDPOLL, COMMON — Brown-streaked bird with red patch above bill and black patch on chin.

SPARROW, SPECIES — Small brown birds with streaked backs; breast may or may not be streaked; comparatively small bill; none of the distinguishing features of our other small winter birds. Two common winter Sparrows have a dark spot on their breast: Song Sparrow on a streaked breast, Tree Sparrow on an unstreaked breast. Illustrated: Song Sparrow.

SPARROW, HOUSE — Common in the city; male told from other Sparrows by black chin patch; female is less streaked, with a buff throat and breast.

CROSSBILL, RED — Dark wings without crossbars; comparatively large bill crossed at its tip; male brick red, female olive green; moves like a parrot, using bill to grasp branches while climbing.

CROSSBILL, WHITE-WINGED — Same as Red Crossbill, except that dark wings are marked with two broad white wing bars. Illustrated: Red Crossbill.

Birds' Nests in Winter

Birds' nests are more obvious in winter than in any other season. What were leafy forms and dense thickets are now merely a few branches, often revealing the once secret spot where a bird built a nest and raised its young.

Birds build nests in the ground, on the ground, in shrubs, in buildings, on and within trees, and on cliffs. The nests we see in winter are only those sturdy enough to last through summer and fall storms, and those not covered by autumn leaves or winter snow. This eliminates by far the majority of nests, which are either built on the ground or are so flimsy that they soon break apart.

Nests most commonly seen are those built below 20 feet above the ground, since we usually concentrate our vision on that range. Good places to look for nests are along the edges of fields and clearings, and among shrubs and low trees. Nests can be spotted by scanning for dark clumps or bunches of material among trees and shrubs. Fresh tree-hole nests can be spotted by finding wood chips on the forest floor, and older tree-hole nests by examining dead standing trees.

Identifying nests in winter has certain drawbacks. One is that neither the birds nor their eggs are present. Another problem is that many of the nests are considerably changed by weathering. This makes certain nests impossible to "pin down" to one particular maker. But there are certain categories of nests which can be easily distinguished from others, and knowing these may lead you to finer distinctions in the future.

Below I have outlined seven characteristic types of nests and in many cases narrowed down to species under each type. The types of nests listed are only those commonly found in winter and do not represent the tremendous variety of summer nests.

General Categories of Nests Commonly Found in Winter

NESTS CONTAINING A LAYER OF MUD; INSIDE DIAMETER ABOUT 4 INCHES

Robin: Lined with grasses, no leaves or sticks in the foundation.

Woodthrush: Lined with rootlets, with leaves in the foundation.

Common Grackle: Lined with grasses, with weed stalks or sticks in the foundation.

LARGE BULKY NEST WITH TWIG AND BARK STRIP FOUNDATION; THICK INNER LINING OF DARK ROOTLETS

Catbird, Mockingbird, Brown Thrasher: These are all similar in foundation and lined with dark rootlets. Brown Thrasher nests are larger than the other two and contain foundation twigs 12 inches long or longer. The Catbird has a tendency to put cellophane in its foundation.

Cardinal: Like the Mockingbird's, not found very far north. It can be distinguished from the others by having no leaves in its foundation and by its lining of grasses instead of rootlets.

These nests are seen most often in shrubs, and frequently used by mice as winter homes, in which case they are lined with Cattail or Milkweed down.

SMALL NESTS NEATLY FORMED OF GRASSES, USUALLY LOWER THAN 3 FEET OFF THE GROUND

Sparrows: Song, Chipping, and Field Sparrows all make small, neatly cupped grass nests, often placing them on the

ground but at other times a few feet off the ground. They are often in the winter weed, Spiraea, and some may be lined with horsehair or, in these days, nylon fishing line.

SMALL NEATLY FORMED NESTS OF MILKWEED OR THISTLE DOWN AND GRASSES, OFTEN IN THE CROTCHES OF SAPLING TREES

Redstart, Yellow Warbler, Goldfinch, Flycatchers: Downy materials show as gray or white in nest foundation. Rain

and weathering greatly alter these nests, making their distinguishing characteristics less clear. Some have quite thick, sturdy walls.

HANGING NESTS SUSPENDED FROM THE TIPS OF BRANCHES

Northern Oriole: Woven of yarn, plant fibers, hair, etcetera, grayish in color, and often hanging from the drooping

branch tips of Elm trees. Outside diameter about 4 inches.

SMALL NESTS NEATLY SUSPENDED AT THEIR RIM TO A FORKING BRANCH

Vireos: Open at the top and built below the branch; outside diameter about 3 inches. Woven with plant fibers and spider silk, lined with pine needles and fine grasses. Nests can be found at any height. More common in woods.

NEST HOLES IN TREES

Chickadees and *Woodpeckers* are known to excavate holes in trees, but many other birds live in these durable homes in following years, such as Titmice, Nuthatches, Wrens, Creepers, Tree Swallows. In larger holes, American Kestrals, Screech Owls, Saw-whet Owls, and Wood Ducks

may nest, as well as Squirrels and Mice. Studies of smaller Woodpecker holes shows that they tend to face east or south and be on the lower side of sloping branches or trunks. These two features enable them to receive the warmth and light of the morning sun and keep rain out.

Natural History Descriptions

Bobwhite (*Colinus virginianus*)

The family life of Bobwhites in summer is close-knit, the young and parents staying together as they roam their territory and feed. In fall, however, the families gather into larger groups, members of families dispersing among the groups. This time is often called the "fall shuffle" and probably insures against too much inbreeding during the coming summer. The larger groups then divide into smaller ones averaging 15 individuals. These are called "coveys"; they remain the social grouping for the rest of the winter.

Each covey eventually establishes its own area or range for feeding. It is a mixed social group of adults and juveniles of both sexes. At night the Bobwhites of a covey arrange themselves into a circular formation, their tails touching in the center, their heads facing outward. Each bird lifts its wings slightly in order to allow warmth to pass between birds. Each night is spent this way, usually in one of several favorite locations. Its function seems to be in protecting the group from cold. Sometimes coveys group into this formation during particularly cold days to conserve warmth and energy. Coveys utilize one of several favorite roosting locations, which can be identified by the ring of droppings the birds leave behind.

It has been shown by experiments that the degree of cold Bobwhites can withstand at night is directly related to the number of birds in the circular formation and that the optimal number is 14 or 15 birds. Often, when a covey becomes reduced by mortality, it will join another in order to increase its number.

Bobwhites, along with Pheasants, Grouse, and Chickens, are gallinaceous birds, a family characterized as ground-feeding, having short beaks and stout bodies, and preferring to walk rather than fly. Bobwhites are ill suited to the cold

Bobwhites

and snow of the north, and yet they are still quite common in the southern half of our snow belt. Their feeding habits are not as adaptable as those of some other northern gallinaceous birds, such as the Ruffed Grouse. During the year Bobwhites feed entirely on insects and seeds, and in winter 95 percent of their diet is seeds. Even a slight snow cover hampers their ability to locate seeds. There is a direct relationship between Bobwhite mortality and the number of consecutive days snow remains on the ground.

Bobwhites prefer a very specific habitat: they need open areas for foraging and brushy areas for cover. Ideal locations are at the edges of fields or pastures, where both situations occur. The size of their winter range depends on the suitability of the environment and the abundance of food — ranges vary from 5 to 75 acres and may overlap slightly with the ranges of other coveys.

As spring comes, individuals pair up and leave the covey.

At this time breeding territories are established, and the familiar "ah-bobwhite" call of the male is commonly heard and enjoyed.

As with each gallinaceous bird, you are more likely to see the tracks than the bird itself. The tracks of Bobwhite will usually be plentiful, for the covey stays fairly close together during the day, and following them may lead you to a winter roosting site. The size and shape of the tracks are shown in the key to the chapter "Tracks in the Snow."

Cardinal (*Cardinalis cardinalis*)

During fall the male Cardinal may not seem as red as usual; he is not. For in late summer Cardinals molt, and many of the male's new feathers are tipped with light gray. As winter wears on, the tips of his feathers wear off, revealing his bright red breeding color beneath.

Female and male Cardinal

Since the 1900s and possibly earlier, the Cardinal has steadily moved north. This gradual migration has been ascribed to the clear trend toward warmer winters recorded over this time. Once strictly a southern bird, now the Cardinal is common in southern New England and parts of southern Canada.

The Cardinal is generally nonmigratory, and records from banding have shown adults to be rarely more than a few miles from their place of birth. Like many of our winter birds, Cardinals gather together in fall, forming loose flocks that stay and feed together. During this time males treat females the same way they treat other males in the flock, but in the second half of winter, males begin to solicit females with song. In late winter the females answer, and as pairs join together, the winter flocks break up.

Cardinal song, like that of most other birds in the Grosbeak family, consists of clear whistles. Both male and female participate in song, sometimes answering each other. Up to 28 distinct calls have been recorded, but among these only a few are commonly heard. The most common is described as "whoit-whoit-whoit-tear, tear, tear." The two parts of this song may be heard separately or together, slowly or extremely fast. Knowing this may help you to identify many of its calls. Another of its common calls is a short "chit . . . chit . . . ," which it seems to use when it is disturbed by another bird or an intruder. Cardinal song may be heard anytime during winter, but especially in late winter and spring, as the breeding season approaches.

The Cardinal's large bill is especially efficient at opening seeds. Attracted to the sunflower seeds at feeders, it takes them in its bill and neatly splits the husk, eating the kernel inside. In the wilds it uses this agility on the seeds of Ashes and Tulip Trees as well as eating seeds in the fruit of Grape, Sumac, and Dogwood berries.

Although most Cardinals join into flocks in winter, some pairs stay alone in their breeding territory. The average size of a flock is about 12 birds, but in the southern part of the Cardinal's winter range the flocks often contain over 50 birds. Flock size depends mainly on the abundance of food and how many birds a certain area can support. This is probably why there are smaller groups in the north, where food is less abundant during winter.

Chickadee, Black-capped (*Parus atricapillus*)

Chickadees are some of the best birds to study in winter. They have interesting behavior and are present all winter in noisy and conspicuous flocks. However, these flocks are not like the loose-knit, free-roaming winter flocks of other birds; they are stable in membership and have rigid social structure. The flocks average 6 birds and form around a dominant pair which bred the previous summer. Other members may be juveniles that may or may not be the young of the dominant pair, as well as a few stray adults. While watching

Chickadees

the flock you may see one bird usurp another's feeding perch by scaring it away. This is a common expression of dominance among birds, and in this case it is an expression of the hierarchical structure of the Chickadee flock.

When out walking you may repeatedly find a Chickadee flock in the same place. This is because a flock will have three to five favorite foraging sites among which it circulates during the day. At these spots the birds feed more intensively than at other areas. These sites define the territory that is defended against other Chickadee flocks, an area that is often an extension of the dominant pair's summer breeding territory. A flock generally has a roosting area within its territory to which the birds return each night; it is often in dense evergreens, but individual birds may roost in small tree holes nearby.

Chickadees have a number of calls which make them easy to locate in the woods. Each call is more or less associated with a certain function. Their most frequent call is their "contact note." This is a high pitched "tseet-tseet" and is continually given by members of the flock in order to keep the flock together. When a bird has strayed farther away it may give the well-known call "chickadee-dee" to locate the flock. A scolding call is given to express dominance within the flock or between flocks; it is just "dee-dee-dee-dee," and is often given when a dominant bird is displacing another from a feeding perch.

The Chickadee has an extraordinary ability to maneuver on branches. It is as comfortable hanging below as it is perching on top. In winter, half of its diet is small eggs or larvae of insects and spiders which are nestled in bark crevices. The rest consists of seeds from Pines and Hemlocks. It has been suggested that the Chickadee's acrobatic ability is an adaptation to winter feeding — when snow covers the tops of evergreen branches, Chickadees can still hang beneath to gather seeds and insects.

In September and October local flocks of Chickadees are augmented by migrant Chickadee flocks. But by November only a few are left, and you have to travel over a number of woodland acres to see or hear a flock. But at this time the flocks begin to be joined by other species, such as Nuthatches, Woodpeckers, Kinglets, Brown Creepers, and Titmice. These are only loose associations, with each species coming and going at different times of day.

Creeper, Brown (*Certhia familiaris*)

The Brown Creeper has been described as a "rather characterless and uninteresting bird," but I find it just the opposite. Unlike the Chickadees and Nuthatches, with their noisy

Brown Creeper

gatherings, the Brown Creeper is inconspicuous and often alone. It is always a treat to discover one as it quietly and industriously hitches itself up a tree trunk, scrutinizing bark crevices for wintering insects.

Its bill is long, thin, and curved, and although unsuited for pecking like the beak of the Nuthatch, it is perfect for reaching around and under bits of bark to glean insect eggs and cocoons. The Brown Creeper is almost completely insectivorous, but by its manner of feeding, reduces its competition for food with the Chickadees, Nuthatches, Kinglets, and Titmice, with whose flocks it is often associated. It is interesting to note that although all of these birds look for food on trees, each one's feeding habits are slightly different from those of the others so that they are not competing as much as one might imagine.

The Creeper climbs trees much as Woodpeckers do, holding onto the bark with its toes and leaning back on its long stiff tail feathers. This way of supporting itself enables it to move easily up the tree. Its characteristic foraging behavior is to alight at the base of a tree and spiral around it as it travels up. Upon reaching a point high up on the tree, it flies to the base of the next tree. Creepers roost either in holes in trees or clinging to bark on a protected area of a tree trunk.

The bird is not much affected by human presence, but when predators such as hawks are near, it flattens itself against the tree trunk, where its brown and white mottled feathers render it practically invisible against the coloring of the bark. In late winter it is not uncommon to find two or more Creepers together, spiraling up trees one after the other, an activity that may be part of their prebreeding display.

Crossbill, Red (*Loxia curvirostra*)
White-winged (*Loxia leucoptera*)

This is one bird which you will see either commonly or not at all, for Red Crossbills are birds of the far North, which move south when cone crops fail.

The crossed bill is an obvious adaptation for prying cone scales apart while the bird's tongue gathers the seeds. The bill would seem to be overspecialized to the point where the birds are at the mercy of the irregular cone crops, but this is not the case. Time and again, observations have proven that Crossbills can adapt to eating both insects and other types of seeds.

The flocks, which are generally large, often feed together

Red Crossbills

in one tree, creating a crackling sound throughout the tree as each bird pries apart cone scales. Then the flock leaves together and moves to the next tree while giving their distinctive call notes. Sometimes they associate with other winter flocks of other birds and, since they are feeding on the ends of the higher branches, they become the "sentries" of the conglomerate flock, warning of approaching danger. Although Crossbills have been observed to be aggressive and competitive in captivity, they are noted for their lack of these characteristics in the wild.

Since the birds always seem to be busy feeding, their distinctive crossed bills may be hard to see, but their feeding habits should help you identify them, for they often use their bills to grab branches as they move, much like a parrot. The Red Crossbill male is brick-red and the female is a mottled greenish yellow. The other species, the White-winged Crossbill, is similar in habits and coloring except that both male and female have two white wing bars.

Crow, Common (*Corvus brachyrhynchos*)

A spectacular feature of Crows in winter is their nightly communal roosts, which in some areas of North America may contain over 200,000 birds apiece. Roosts near you can be located by watching the direction toward which groups of Crows are flying in late afternoon or the direction from which they come at dawn, for every morning the birds disperse from their roost in small groups to feed, and then return at sunset in the same way. Why they roost together in such huge flocks is unknown. The roosts are usually located near good winter feeding grounds, such as by the ocean at river deltas, or near large inland lakes, but availability of food does not explain the size of the roosts.

Most Crows that summer in Canada or northern New England migrate south, for the northern snow cover makes feeding difficult. But many still remain and may drift to roosts by the sea or the Great Lakes or near large city dumps. These northern roosts are much smaller than those found farther south and will most likely contain between 500 and 10,000 birds.

Crows

Crows are seasoned omnivores, and will take advantage of any food source. At least 50 percent of Crows' winter diet is corn, the kernels that remain in the fields after harvesting. About 25 percent is other grains, weed seeds, and wild fruits, and the last 25 percent is animal matter collected near water, carrion found along roadsides, and garbage from town dumps. What remains undigested in the Crow's stomach is collected into a pellet and regurgitated. These pellets can be easily found under the roosts and are often clues to the bird's diet. In one study of a winter roost, it was found that the pellets consisted mostly of seeds. They averaged 36 seeds from either poison ivy or poison sumac, and many other seeds from Sumac, Grape, Dogwood, Hackberry, and Buckthorn.

As Crows feed in small groups, often one or more will stay on a perch and warn those feeding of approaching danger. Crows are extremely vocal and will always harass Owls or Hawks that they have spotted. If you see Crows swarming around a tree, it is worthwhile approaching, for you may locate an Owl or Hawk.

Since Crows do most of their feeding on land their footprints are a common sight. They sometimes hop, but more usually they walk. Their track pattern is easily identified and often has a characteristic mark where the bird drags the toe of its foot between each print and the next. At the landing or takeoff point of the trail you may see the beautiful imprint of the bird's wings at either side of its feet. Good places for Crow tracks are in cultivated fields and the snow-covered surfaces of frozen lakes.

Dove, Mourning (*Zenaida macroura*)

The Mourning Dove is a ground feeding bird related to our domestic Pigeon. During winter, the doves gather in large flocks, which feed and roost as units. Seeds from grasses, corn, and weeds, and the berries from Pokeweed are important items in its strictly vegetarian diet. The birds are not

Mourning Doves

strong enough to scratch through crusted snow for their food, therefore most migrate south; but many others still manage to remain as winter residents in areas of intermittent snow cover.

When you approach a flock, they will all fly up into trees nearby; they can be recognized by the whistling sound their wings make as they take off. In level flight, they are spectacular fliers, their wings bending back after each powerful stroke and their pointed tails streaming behind.

Their name, which until seen in print is often thought to be "Morning Dove," refers to their song, which consists of five "coos," the second one rising and falling in tone; it is definitely a mournful sound. The call, so common at other times of year, most likely won't be heard in winter. But in spring, as the flocks break up and pairing begins, the call is often heard.

Dove, Rock (*Columba livia*)

The Rock Dove, or Pigeon, is an excellent and beautiful flyer. It seems awkward at times on land, but once it is in

Rock Doves, or Pigeons

the air, its agility is remarkable. In flocks, Rock Doves display a marvelous ability for simultaneous flight as they circle and rise in unison. Strong flight is undoubtedly an adaptation to their native habitat, which is on the edges of cliffs by the sea. Here, with their nests on ledges and within caves, the birds had to be excellent flyers both to land on their perches and to contend with the changing gusts of wind so common along ocean cliffs.

The birds are not native to North America but were brought here as domesticated birds by European settlers. In time, many of the birds escaped or were released and started breeding. As cities grew up, Rock Doves were comfortable with the tall buildings that were so similar to their rocky cliffs; they now commonly place their nests on window ledges and air conditioners and among the crannies of bridges.

In the cities Pigeons feed mostly on garbage and human handouts. When near parks they feed on grass and weed seeds, never scratching the ground for them but only gleaning those that are in plain sight. During breeding season they are often in pairs, but for the winter months they simply gather in large flocks.

Ducks, Mallard (*Anas platyrhynchos*)
Black (*Anas rubripes*)

Almost everyone has had an occasion to watch Mallards or Black Ducks swim lazily around a park pond, but how many have seen their fascinating courtship displays, which occur most frequently during the months of November and December, continuing at a lower intensity throughout winter? Here is a chance for even experienced birdwatchers to discover new things about old birds, and of all places, in the local duck pond.

Different displays are done by females and males. The most common display of females is called "inciting." The female swims after the male of her choice and repeatedly nods her head back over her shoulder. This display has been called an "avowal of love" and may signify her choice of a mate. To see this, watch pairs where the female is following.

The bulk of the rest of the displays is done by groups of males toward each other. First the males do "preliminary shaking." A male floats with his head compressed down on his neck, so much so that on a Mallard the white ring on the neck does not show. After holding like this for a minute or two, the male lifts its head slightly and tentatively shakes it. It stops and repeats the shaking two more times, each time shaking more vigorously. Other nearby males usually do this also.

This display is not striking and may go unnoticed at first.

Male and female Mallard

It may occur as an isolated incident or may be followed by a series of other displays.

After preliminary shaking, a female may swim quickly around and among the males, jerking her head up, then down and stretched out flat along the water. This is "nod-swimming" and tends to stimulate the males to continue with other displays. It is very obvious and may help draw your attention to the following more subtle behavior of the males.

After the nod-swimming of the female the males may do one of three different displays, each of which is accompanied by a short whistle easily heard on a still day. One of these male displays, the "grunt-whistle," consists of the duck lifting the back of its neck high in the air while keeping its bill and tail in the water; at the same time it gives a grunt and whistle, but only the whistle is easily heard.

Mated pairs also display together. The male and female ducks face each other and alternately jerk their heads downward. This is called "pumping" and can be preliminary to mating, where the male swims onto the back of the female and holds the feathers from the back of her head in his bill. Mating can be followed by male nod-swimming.

These displays are best seen on a still day when the ducks are through with intensive feeding. Sometimes a slight disturbance, such as shooing those on land into water, can stimulate certain displays to occur.

Finch, Purple (*Carpodacus purpureus*)

A common bird at suburban feeders in winter is the Purple Finch. You may at first mistake the bird for a sparrow, but the raspberry-colored feathers on the head and breast of the male and the large conical bill on the brown and white streaked female clearly distinguish it. The Purple Finch breeds in northern Canada and joins others in flocks to mi-

Male and female Purple Finches

grate south for the winter. Often females will arrive a few weeks ahead of the males.

Although gregarious in winter, it is quite aggressive toward its own species when feeding, but still Purple Finches roost together at night, generally in dense evergreens. In the wild they are often seen with groups of Goldfinches, feeding on the seeds of winter weeds. When seeds are scarce they eat Maple and Birch buds and the fruits of shrubs. In fact, their generic name, *Carpodacus*, means "fruit-biting" and may refer to their habit of eating buds off fruit trees as well as pecking at the fruit in fall.

Purple Finches are well-known for their song, which is a long, rich, and variable warble.

Goldfinch, American (*Spinus tristis*)

After breeding in late summer male Goldfinches molt their bright yellow feathers, replacing them with muted yellow-green plumage that resembles the female plumage. In winter, they typically gather in flocks of from 5 to 100 birds, feeding on the grass and weed seeds of fields. Some of their more favorite foods are the seeds from Ragweed, Thistles, Goldenrod, Evening Primrose, and Mullein. Goldfinches often are joined by flocks of other birds that have similar feeding habits, such as the Tree Sparrows when in fields and Pine Siskins and Common Redpolls when feeding among conifers.

Goldfinches have a characteristic flight, which resembles the line created by a loose wire draped between telephone poles. The bird flies up, then, holding its wings against its body, swoops down, then again flies up. It characteristically gives a twittering call as it flies.

The Goldfinch is one of our latest breeders, waiting until late summer or early fall, when it uses the down from the matured thistle seeds to construct its nest. As a result the nest is often in better shape in winter than those of birds

Goldfinches

that bred in early spring and whose nests may have already been torn apart by summer and fall storms. See the key to bird's nests for help in identifying it.

Grosbeak, Evening (*Hesperiphona vespertina*)

The Evening Grosbeak is a beautiful winter bird that is becoming more and more common in eastern Canada and northeastern states. Originally it was only a northwestern bird, but has extended its range eastward in the last forty years. When you spot Evening Grosbeaks in the wild, they will either be in calling flocks overhead or feeding on seeds in the tops of Maple, Locust, or Ash trees. Later in winter they frequent the ground, looking for fallen seeds, or come

Evening Grosbeaks

to feeders, where they are often belligerent toward their own and other species.

Like all Grosbeaks, they have bills that are particularly well adapted to feeding on seeds and are even strong enough to crack cherry pits to get at the nourishment inside. Although they eat some insects in summer, they are strict vegetarians in winter.

Their colors are particularly striking. The white and black patches of their wings, the yellow area on the male's forehead, and their large whitened conical bills are all easily seen, as the birds are not generally frightened by human presence.

Grosbeak, Pine (*Pinicola enucleator*)

Although not as blatantly red as the Cardinal, the Pine Grosbeak is our largest red winter bird. But the two are not likely to be confused, for while the Cardinal is a southern bird extending its range to the north, the Pine Grosbeak is

Pine Grosbeaks

decidedly northern and barely makes it as far south as the United States in winter. Not until after December does it regularly cross Canada's southern border. But in the provinces it is locally common, and quite tame, feeding especially on Pine and Maple seeds and the berries from Mountain Ash.

The Pine Grosbeak is one of our winter birds that have worldwide distribution, for this same species is common in northern Europe, European Russia, and Siberia, and its range in North America extends across the continent all the way to Alaska.

Grouse, Ruffed (*Bonasa umbellus*)
Spruce (*Canachites canadensis*)

Two species of Grouse live in the area covered by this guide: the Spruce Grouse and the Ruffed Grouse.

The Ruffed Grouse spends most of its time on the ground,

Ruffed Grouse

and you will probably see its tracks many times before actually seeing the bird. Its feet are physically adapted for travel on snow. In fall, small comblike projections grow on either side of the toes, doubling the surface area of the feet and supporting them on soft snow. Their growth is believed to be stimulated by the photoperiod of the fall days; the combs are shed again in the spring.

The tracks of the Ruffed Grouse may lead you to one of its winter roosts. When the snow conditions are right, the bird takes advantage of the insulating qualities of snow by burrowing beneath it for the night. It either scratches out a cavity or dives from above into soft snow, then tunnels a short distance and remains there for the night. The tunnels can be clearly recognized, for the bird always leaves droppings, small cylindrical scats about one inch long composed of plant fibers. Often tracks and wing imprints of the bird's landing or taking off can be seen around these snow roosts.

Unlike our other gallinaceous birds, the Bobwhite and Ring-necked Pheasant, Ruffed Grouse prefer to stay in the woods and in winter eat only plant material, mostly tree buds from Aspen, Oak, Hawthorn, and Beech, but also beechnuts, acorns, and the leaves from Mountain Laurel.

In contrast to this diet, the Spruce Grouse eats almost entirely buds from Pines, Spruces, and Firs. It is also a more sedentary bird, often spending a day or two in one evergreen tree, eating in daytime and roosting there at night. The Spruce Grouse is extremely tame, allowing humans to approach within a few feet and still remaining unconcerned. It lives farther north than the Ruffed Grouse and in southern latitudes will be found only in the mountains.

To distinguish Grouse tracks from those of Pheasant and Bobwhite, consult the key in Chapter 7.

Gulls (*Larus* species)

Although many Gulls (largely immature) migrate south in fall, the adults tend to shift to river valleys, the seacoast, and the Great Lakes region. By spending winter in these areas the Gulls can continue to find food at the water's exposed edge. Besides these natural areas, Gulls also congregate at town and city dumps, where they eagerly await the tidbits of food that arrive in the new refuse.

But Gulls were well adapted to the omnivorous diet of the scavenger long before dumps became as large as they are today, for their natural habitat skirts the edges of two radically different environments: the land and the sea. In order to exploit the coastal edge, the Gull has become generalized in physiology and adaptable in habit. Its wings are neither as large as those of true sea birds nor as agile as land birds'. Its feet are webbed and it can swim, but it also walks easily and does most of its foraging on land. And compared to other birds', a Gull's bill is quite unspecialized.

These all enable the Gull to take advantage of many sources of food. Gulls feed on such varied items as earthworms, fish, rodents, mollusks, insects, and other birds' eggs. The Gull has a huge crop, which easily contains whole rats or fish that they might catch, and like many other large birds they regurgitate the undigestible parts of their food, in the form of small pellets about one inch long.

Herring Gulls

Gulls are generally gregarious at all times of the year. In winter they are most often seen in flocks that are traveling between roosting grounds and feeding sites. The roosting grounds are usually in open areas such as the centers of coastal bays, or remote beaches along the coast. When coastal weather is bad, they move inland and roost in open fields.

There are three common winter gulls in the northeastern and north central area. The largest is the Great Black-backed Gull, easily recognized by its black back and wing tops. The next in size is the Herring Gull, undoubtedly the most common of all our Gulls. Its appearance is generally nondescript, gray and white. The smallest, the Ring-billed Gull, is similar to the Herring Gull except that it is smaller and has a black ring that encircles its bill just in from the tip. All of these Gulls when one or two years old have an immature plumage that is mottled white and brown. To distinguish immature species, either consult a more detailed bird guide or else be content to know that all brownish gulls are still immature.

A great deal has been discovered about the behavior of Gulls, especially regarding their particular postures and stances that communicate social messages. Unfortunately, this behavior is limited primarily to the breeding season and would only rarely be observed in winter.

Hawks (*Circus hudsonicus, Buteo* species, *Falco* species)

If during the day in winter you see soaring overhead a bird that is neither a Crow nor a Gull, then you have most likely spotted a Hawk. Hawks are large day-hunting birds that kill prey with the talons on their feet. Since their main diet is the Meadow Vole, they are most often seen hunting over fields and large open areas.

Almost all small mammals and birds are instantly aware

Red-tailed Hawk

of the presence of Hawks. Birds seek the cover of trees, and mammals freeze or run to their burrows. By their hunting methods Hawks try to offset this awareness on the part of their prey.

There are at least four common ways Hawks hunt, and often a species can be recognized by observing the way it hunts. Marsh Hawks hunt low to the ground, soaring just over the tops of grasses and shrubs. They depend on coming suddenly upon their prey and catching it unaware.

American Kestrels and Rough-legged Hawks hover in midair over fields, waiting for their prey to reemerge; then they dive down on it. The Red-tailed Hawk and Red-shouldered Hawk also wait, but they sit motionless in dead trees by the side of a field, or circle high overhead. When they spot prey, they coast off their perch or dive to attack.

When circling overhead, sometimes Hawks soar so high that they are only specks in the sky. Their eyesight is still so good that they can easily spot mice below and dive down upon them at tremendous speeds.

Between 75 percent and 95 percent of Hawk prey in winter consists of Meadow Voles, depending on the species of Hawk. The next most common prey animal is the White-footed Mouse, and it averages almost 10 percent of the diet. The rest of the diet is made up of larger mammals and small birds. Hawks usually pluck the fur or feathers off their prey before eating pieces of it whole. Many of the bones are eaten, and these, along with some fur, are regurgitated in the form of pellets. These pellets often accumulate under a roosting perch. By breaking them apart you can often discover the complete skulls and teeth of the rodents the Hawks have eaten.

Since the availability of prey depends heavily on the amount of snow cover, most Hawks migrate south, to where snow cover is at least intermittent. Of those that remain in the north the most common will be the Red-tailed Hawk, Red-shouldered Hawk, Marsh Hawk, and the American Kestrel.

Jay, Blue (*Cyanocitta cristata*)
Gray (*Perisoreus canadensis*)

Even more than Crows, Jays seem to take on the role of sentinel in nature. It is a rare moment when you can watch

Blue Jay

a Jay going quietly about its activities, for at most times it will spot you and sound "alarm" or "assembly" calls, which cause other Jays to join in warning all the rest of nature of your presence. Jays are particularly aggressive toward natural predators of the Dog, Cat, or Weasel families as well as toward Hawks and Owls. Their typical alarm or assembly call is the familiar "jaaay, jaaay."

Throughout the year Jays are aggressive food gatherers. They eat whatever they can get and often store food either in the ground or in crevices of the trunks and branches of trees. Their storing habits are irregular: sometimes they collect acorns in a knothole only to take them out for eating a few minutes later; at other times, food is carefully stored and left to rot or for squirrels to steal.

The Gray Jay of Canada and the northern states has gen-

Gray Jay

eral habits similar to those of the Blue Jay — storing food, having a variety of social calls, and being aggressive toward intruders — but its winter flocking habits may differ substantially. They have not yet been carefully studied. The Gray Jay does start nesting earlier than the Blue Jay, often building its nest and incubating eggs while snow is still on the ground.

Junco, Dark-eyed (*Junco hyemalis*)

Juncos breed in the northern coniferous woods but migrate south in fall, spending the winter anywhere between southern Canada and the Gulf of Mexico. They winter in parks and suburbs of the city as well as in the country and often feed in the company of other birds, especially House Sparrows in the city and Tree Sparrows in the country.

Juncos migrate in small flocks. Each flock upon arrival establishes four or five favorite foraging sites, usually no more than two to three hundred yards apart. Members of this flock feed only at these established sites; they may forage alone or with different combinations of members of their flock, but rarely as a whole group. As new Juncos arrive they may join this flock by participating in its circuit of feeding sites.

It has also been shown, by banding the birds, that many individuals return to the same winter area each year, showing an ability to home in on winter areas as well as to summer breeding grounds. The first winter arrivals are often birds that have been there in previous winters, birds already

Dark-eyed Juncos

familiar with the foraging sites. Later arrivals may be younger birds, which are then integrated into the habits of the older flock.

Juncos are lovely winter birds and relatively unafraid of humans. They are unmistakable as they fly away, for their gray tails are lined on either side with white feathers. They feed primarily on seeds, especially Ragweed in the city. Their paired tracks are common, since they do most of their foraging on the ground.

In late winter before the flocks break up and individuals migrate north, you will hear a new bird song in the air. It is a high sustained trill, and it is the song of the Junco, which hasn't done more than twitter all winter. The call is one associated with its breeding period and probably signals to us the imminence of their spring migration.

Kinglet, Golden-crowned (*Regulus satrapa*)
Ruby-crowned (*Regulus calendula*)

The Kinglet is the smallest bird of the winter woods, from beak to tail only 3½ inches long. It migrates down from the

Golden-crowned Kinglets

north in small flocks, most often feeding in Pines or Spruces. Its thin pointed bill is a mark of its insectivorous habits as it flits about the trees feeding on insect eggs and wintering spiders. Kinglets are so tame that it is common to be within ten feet of their active feeding. The yellow strip on the top of the heads of Golden-crowned Kinglets is often visible and makes them like little jewels of the winter woods.

Their flocks are often accompanied by a Downy Woodpecker or two and Chickadees. Its relative, the Ruby-crowned Kinglet, winters more to the south, but the two may be seen together in the north along the coast. The Golden-crowned Kinglet flocks in winter utilize contact notes to keep the flock together. This note can be recognized simply because it is the highest and slightest note one can imagine.

Lark, Horned (*Eremophila alpestris*)

After leaving the nest, immature Horned Larks join together into flocks. In August and September the adults join them,

Horned Larks

and these flocks of from 10 to 100 birds stay together for the winter. Horned Larks have a decided preference for open barren areas. In this habitat they both feed and roost during winter and will nest in similar areas in spring. Common places to see them are barren land by the shore, open fields, and the large median strips of turnpikes. They feed on grass seeds, and their flocks are sometimes joined by Lapland Longspurs, sparrowlike birds from the far north. At night they roost in the same barren areas, settling out of the wind under tufts of grass.

Mockingbird (*Mimus polyglottus*)

You must get out in early fall to see the interesting behavior of Mockingbirds. The stages of territory establishment can occur very quickly, and once they have been completed, Mockingbirds are quiet and inconspicuous for the rest of the winter. In early fall, many Mockingbirds may gather in favorable winter locations, "favor" being determined by the amount of available berries and fruit. During this time there will seem to be interminable chasing of birds from one bush or tree to another with no apparent consistent dominance by one bird. All chasing and aggression is usually accompanied by a loud "chewk . . . chewk" call. Mockingbirds will also be heard singing their continuous imitations of other birds' songs, usually each phrase repeated three times.

Soon, Mockingbirds pick prominent perches on the tops of small trees or shrubs and claim a few of these perches as the border markers of their territory. If a stray Mockingbird enters the area, each of the settled birds will start singing and "chewk"-ing and will chase the stray bird away.

The final stage of territory marking is inconspicuous but should be looked for. Where two territories abut, the two "owners" will land on the ground at the boundary line. They face each other, their tails pointed up, and hop forward and backward and from side to side. At the conclusion, both

Mockingbird

birds fly off into their territories. In late fall Mockingbirds will also chase other species out of their territory, especially migrating Robins and Cedar Waxwings, which also eat berries.

After about two months of activity in fall, Mockingbirds radically change their behavior; they become quiet and secretive, no longer singing or using their perches but merely skulking within the cover of their territory, for after early winter the territories seem agreed upon and there is no need for display.

The territories may be held by a pair or a single male or female bird. Sometimes a pair that bred last spring will hold separate but adjacent territories in winter. In the south, Mockingbirds are known for inhabiting the cities. This is also increasingly true in the north. Suburbs are probably good wintering areas for the birds because of extensive planting of shrubs.

Nuthatch, White-breasted (*Sitta carolinensis*)
Red-breasted (*Sitta canadensis*)

Although Nuthatches are not numerous you will nonetheless probably see them in winter, for they are often in the company of noisy Chickadee flocks and they are relatively tame toward humans. The Nuthatch is our only winter bird that can climb down a tree. Other trunk climbers such as the Brown Creeper and the Woodpeckers generally rely on sitting back on their tail feathers for support and usually face upward. But the Nuthatch just holds on hard with its feet and wanders up and down tree trunks at whim. This may give it some slight advantage in finding insects that Creepers and Woodpeckers missed coming the other way.

But the main food of the Nuthatch in winter is nuts: acorns, beechnuts, hickory nuts, and the pits from cherries. It is able to break open many of these to get at the nut, often wedging them into tree crevices in order to peck harder at them. Closely related to this same behavior of bracing nuts in crevices is its habit of storing food. In fall, Nuthatches take Hemlock seeds and bits of nuts from their source and store them in among bark crevices for later use.

White-breasted Nuthatch

There have even been observations of Nuthatches "covering" these stores with bits of bark or lichens.

Both male and female Nuthatches remain in the same territory year round, and because they do, they tend to select the same mates year after year. The territories are large and may in part be extended by an even larger range. These tend to become established over the years, and this fact, along with their size, results in very little aggressive behavior over territory boundaries. Within the territory the male and female have separate roosts. These roosts are holes in trees, holes probably chiseled out by a Downy or Hairy Woodpecker. Downies have been observed to take over the roost of a Nuthatch and vice versa. But since the Nuthatch seems to prefer a larger roost-hole entrance, there is probably no serious competition between the two.

In late winter Nuthatches begin their courtship song and display. These take place mostly within an hour after the male leaves his roost hole in the morning. They are subtle and not easily seen and so not included in this account. But the common call of the Nuthatch is not subtle and is easily heard. It is a nasal "ank . . . ank . . . ank" and is the best way to locate the bird.

Owls (Order *Strigiformes*)

Owls and Hawks are our two main birds of prey. While Hawks hunt only by day, Owls hunt mostly at night. They have large eyes, which help them see at night, but they also depend mostly on their ears to pinpoint the rustlings of small rodents among the grasses and leaves. Their flight is quieter than that of most birds because of the construction of their flight feathers, so no extra sound is made that might warn prey of their attack.

Owls eat primarily rodents and thus perform a valuable function in helping control mouse populations. The larger Owls also feed on small mammals such as Hares, Squirrels,

Great Horned Owl

and Skunks; the smaller Owls feed occasionally on small birds and in summer on insects. Birds are often plucked of their feathers before being eaten, but many mice are just eaten whole. The undigested remains of fur and bones are then coughed back up as dense pellets, similar to those of Hawks. The "castings" can be found under nests or places where the Owls roost during daytime. (Crows and Gulls also cough up castings.)

One of the largest and most commonly seen Owls is the Great Horned Owl. It has become adapted to living in suburbs. It usually sits quietly among evergreens during the day but is frequently mobbed by Crows, which force it to shift continually from tree to tree, trying to rid itself of their calls and attacks. Other Owls, such as the Short-eared Owl and Snowy Owl, prefer to nest and roost on the ground in open areas. The Snowy Owl is a spectacular bird that comes south from the Arctic in winter. It is mostly white and blends with the snow as it sits on the ground in open areas.

Pheasant, Ring-necked (*Phasianus colchicus*)

The Pheasant is basically a ground-dwelling bird. It will skulk away from you into the underbrush if it can, but if you get too close it will flush into flight, climbing steeply for a short distance, then spreading its wings and gliding slowly down. You may have seen a pheasant gliding above you across a road or turnpike after it was flushed from one side.

Because of its terrestrial nature you are more likely to see its tracks than the bird itself, and through tracking you can observe some of the Pheasant's more interesting winter habits. Pheasants join together in fall and winter in flocks of anywhere from 4 to over a hundred birds, mostly averaging about 15 birds per flock. The ratio of females to males in these flocks is about 3:1, which reflects the "harem" breeding behavior of Pheasants in spring. The flocks feed and roost together. Roosts are usually in lowland swamps, where cattails and other vegetation provide both cover and insulation. The flocks feed in the morning and evening but are known to stay in their roosts if the weather is severe. Their favorite winter food is field corn, so Pheasants are most abundant in farm areas with scrub field edges.

The size of Pheasant flocks is dependent on the abundance of food and suitable roosting cover. During winter

Male and female Ring-necked Pheasants

thaws, and as spring approaches, the swamps melt and force the birds to find other roosting areas. There is minimal cover at this time, which makes them more vulnerable to predator attack, especially by Hawks, Owls, and Foxes.

Actually, the Ring-necked Pheasant is not a native of North America. It is a hybrid whose original strain comes from China. It was first introduced in New Hampshire in 1790 by the governor of the state. The Pheasants soon died, but in 1880 and 1890 Pheasants were sent from Shanghai to Oregon, where they were released and succeeded in breeding and adjusting. Today the Ring-necked Pheasant lives all across North America and has learned to take advantage of numerous habitats; I have even scared them up from railroad yards in city centers.

Redpoll, Common (*Acanthis flammea*)

The Common Redpoll comes from its breeding grounds at the edge of the Canadian tundra south to the northern

Common Redpolls

states for the winter. It is usually in flocks of from 5 to 50 birds and, like its relatives, the American Goldfinch and Pine Siskin, feeds in ever-active flocks on seeds from weeds and trees. Common Redpolls are known to favor particularly Alder and Birch groves, both trees producing abundant supplies of seeds that remain in winter. The further north you go the more you can expect to see their isolated flocks, for they prefer to stay as close to the tundra edge as weather and food permits.

They are smaller than the Purple Finch and both sexes have a well-defined patch on their crown. The Redpoll's black chin clearly distinguishes it from the Goldfinch, Pine Siskin, or House Finch, with which it might be confused.

Siskin, Pine (*Spinus pinus*)

The Pine Siskin is another of the winter finches with the winter flocking habits of its relative the Goldfinch. Large

Pine Siskin

flocks of from 10 to 100 birds fly and feed together in compact groups. Their food in winter consists of seeds from Hemlock, Alder, Birch, and various weeds. They sometimes feed with American Goldfinches or Common Redpolls.

Their appearance has no consistently striking features, but they can be told from other small brown streaked birds by their longer pointed bills. In flight yellow patches may show on the tops of the wings and base of the tail. Their call is helpful in identifying them and has been described as similar to the sound of "steam escaping from a radiator."

Sparrow, House (*Passer domesticus*)

The House Sparrow is separated here from other sparrows because it is not a native of North America and not a relative of our native Sparrows. It belongs to a family of birds called Weaver Finches or *Ploceidae*. It was introduced into this country in 1850 and 1851 with the hope that it might control some insect pests. The birds were released in Brooklyn, New York, and now are widespread over North America, inhabiting all but the deserts and highest mountains.

They are aggressive little birds and many believe they have driven some of our native birds away from the city and countryside. They are particularly successful in the city, nesting in and on buildings and living off the crumbs of civilization as well as monopolizing our bird feeders at the expense of some of our small native birds.

The male after its fall molt has a mottled breast. But by late winter the tips of the feathers have worn off, revealing a sleek black bib underneath. The female is a soft brown in coloration.

House Sparrows feed together in winter in small flocks. They like to feed at the edges of fields or where shrubs are near, so that at the least sign of danger they can all fly up together into the shrubbery for protection. Then one by one they will begin to return to feeding. Sometimes the flock

House Sparrows

will stop feeding and just sit in nearby shrubs preening and chattering.

They often roost together in ivy-covered walls, but in colder weather they roost singly in the niches and corners of buildings.

Sparrow, Song (*Melospiza melodia*)
Tree (*Spizella arborea*)

Sparrows are small brown birds that feed on seeds in shrubby open areas. In summer the number of species and their similar coloring are discouraging to most beginners, but in winter almost all of these species fly south, allowing us to identify more easily those that remain. One of these, the Tree Sparrow, summers in northern Canada, and so the only chance to see it is in winter when it migrates to southern Canada and the northern states. It is easily recognized by the dark spot on the middle of its clear gray breast and by its rufous cap. It gathers in winter flocks, which are often seen feeding with Junco flocks. Their primary food in winter is grass seeds.

Another common sparrow living in the range of this guide

Song Sparrows

is the Song Sparrow. It, too, has a dot on its breast, but its breast is heavily streaked with brown, and the dot is irregular in shape. Most migrate south in winter, but a few remain, sometimes gathering in small groups near the coast, or by marshes or fields where food is abundant. They also feed on the seeds from grasses and weeds in winter.

Other types of Sparrows can be expected to be seen in the north along the coast, for the sea has a moderating effect on the environment and is a good source of food. These include the Field Sparrow, White-throated Sparrow, Swamp Sparrow, and Fox Sparrow. Most of them are found only along the coast north to Massachusetts and further inland in the south, starting at Pennsylvania.

Starling (*Sturnus vulgaris*)

Like the Crow, the Starling also gathers in huge numbers, sometimes between 50,000 and 250,000 birds, to roost. The locations may be used for more than one winter, but usually the birds' droppings kill all vegetation and their weight on trees breaks the branches, so that the site is no longer suitable. Starlings start gathering for their roost about one or two hours before sunset, usually staying first in small groups near the roost. These small groups join others that are circling the area, and finally as a large group they fly over the roost and suddenly dive into its center. The birds, singing together in the roost, sound from a distance like a tremendous waterfall.

In morning the birds fly up by the thousands, and, sorting themselves into smaller flocks, then disperse to feed. As with those of Crows, these roosts can be located by noting the direction in which flocks of Starlings are traveling at dawn or dusk.

Over winter the Starling's appearance changes considerably. Around September the bird molts, and the new feathers, everywhere but on its back, are all tipped with white. The bird keeps this speckled appearance until midwinter, when the white tips begin to wear off and reveal the bird's glossy black plumage. Also at this time the Starling's bill, which has been dark since its molt, now changes to bright yellow. This latter change occurs just before breeding activity begins — usually in January or February.

Starlings

Starlings are among our most efficient predators of ground insects. They feed in flocks of a hundred or more birds in winter and prefer large open areas such as city parks, cultivated fields, and the borders of large turnpikes. They feed in a close group, all moving in the same direction. The ones at the back periodically fly to the front. When disturbed, they all fly up and in simultaneous flight wheel around, then again land to resume feeding. Studies of their feeding habits have suggested that they may have the ability to adopt the feeding habits of other species of birds that join them.

The Starling is not all beneficial, though, by any account. Introduced from Europe into Central Park, New York City, in 1890 and 1891, it quickly took over in the city and rapidly spread across the country. It is aggressive and nests in holes, depriving many of our native birds of their nesting and roosting sites. Its roosting in cities and feeding at airports have caused major problems in some areas. The numbers of Starlings have not stopped increasing since it was introduced. It will be interesting to see if there is some natural check on their population growth, for though humans introduced the Starling, we seem helpless to stop its spreading.

Titmouse, Tufted (*Parus bicolor*)

The Tufted Titmouse is generally a permanent resident of the areas it inhabits. It is often seen in small flocks of from 3 to 6 birds, and these flocks generally stay within a given range, not overlapping with the ranges of other Titmouse flocks. The flocks often consist of parents with their young, which then split up in spring. Titmice are often part of larger mixed-species flocks in winter. Studies of these mixed foraging flocks show that either Chickadees or Titmice tend to be the leaders in directing the movement of the flock as a whole. Other birds seen in the flocks include Creepers, Nuthatches, Chickadees, Kinglets, and Woodpeckers.

Tufted Titmice

Titmice are some of the more vocal birds of winter. They seem to be continually chattering a series of unmusical notes, often sounding remarkably like Chickadees. Toward the end of winter you are more likely to hear their clear whistle of two notes slurred together, like "peter — peter — peter," and these, when slurred even more into "peer — peer — peer," resemble the notes of the Cardinal. By imitating this call, you can nearly always get the bird to stop what it's doing and come look for its competition.

Although their summer food is primarily insects, the winter food of Titmice is chiefly acorns, beechnuts, corn, and some wild berries. They also glean the limbs of trees for small wintering insects. Titmice have been known occasionally to store food in crevices much as the Nuthatches do but not nearly as often.

The Tufted Titmouse used to be a strictly southern bird, but with the apparent trend toward milder weather and the popularity of bird feeders, it is continually extending its northern range.

Winter's Birds and Abandoned Nests / **243**

Woodpecker, Downy (*Dendrocopos pubescens*)
Hairy (*Dendrocopos villosus*)

Hairy Woodpeckers and Downy Woodpeckers are similar in appearance but differ widely in their winter habits. Hairy Woodpeckers can be distinguished by the size of their bills, which are at least as long as their heads from front to back. Downy Woodpecker bills are much smaller. The males of both species have red on the back of their heads; the females don't.

Hairy Woodpeckers do not migrate, and a mated pair will keep the same territory for life. They begin courtship display in midwinter and continue to establish their bond until mating. The male takes the initiative in the display.

Some Downy Woodpeckers migrate south, but many still remain north. The male is generally aggressive toward the female until late winter. In March and April the female takes the initiative in courtship display, attracting a mate, and choosing a territory.

Both species use "signal posts," particularly resonant trees

Downy Woodpecker

on which they "drum" to announce territory, attract a mate, or establish pair bonds. This drumming serves many of the functions song does in other birds. Usually both male and female have separate posts, each of which is strategically located within the territory. Locating these posts can help you to estimate the extent of a Woodpecker's territory. Near them there may also be good places to observe their behavior. Drumming may begin as early as December and it continues until summer.

Woodpeckers roost at night in separate roosting holes. These are found or excavated in fall and often vigorously defended against other hole-roosting birds. The larger range of the birds, averaging five to eight acres depending on habitat, is not defended but acts like a buffer zone around a roost or nest hole. Although each species does not nest near its own kind, it will tolerate other species of Woodpeckers within its territory. Thus the activities of Hairy and Downy Woodpeckers may overlap considerably.

Woodpeckers eat insects that live under the bark in the wood of trees. Each type of Woodpecker makes holes of a slightly different shape when looking for food. The two most conspicuous foraging holes are those made by Sapsuckers and Pileated Woodpeckers. Sapsuckers make rings of evenly spaced holes around a trunk. They drink the sap and eat the insects that are attracted to it. The holes are about ¼ inch in diameter and form easily recognizable geometric patterns. They are often seen on Apple trees.

The Pileated Woodpecker is huge for a Woodpecker, more than twice as large as the Hairy Woodpecker. The bird eats primarily carpenter ants inside trees. To get at them it chisels huge holes out of dead or living trees, holes that can be as much as 6 feet long, 8 inches wide, and 6 inches deep. The holes are always straight-sided and are far more conspicuous than the bird, which is shy and retiring.

VI

Mushrooms in Winter

W<small>HO WOULD THINK</small> that, in winter, dead tree trunks, fallen logs, and rotting stumps could be exciting places to explore? But they are, for it is here that you will discover the many beautiful varieties of "Bracket" Fungi. It is a familiar theme in nature that where there is death there is likely to be a concentration of life, for in death the complex substances of a living organism are released and made available as nutrients to other plants and animals. This is also true of the Bracket Fungi; they grow on dead wood, using the nutrients that the roots and green leaves of the living tree once collected.

Bracket Fungi are a type of mushroom. But they don't look like the mushrooms we buy in stores or find growing in lawns. They are usually semicircular, tough, and leathery, and broadly attached to living or dead trees. In many cases they grow in clusters, one above the other, covering whole sides of trees.

There are only a few kinds that are really common in our area, and they can be distinguished quite easily. Some have beautiful upper surfaces, many have striking lower surfaces, some form spectacular groupings, others are impressive as lone forms. But, in any case, the part we see and identify is only a portion of the plant. The rest is within the wood, causing decay perhaps growing inside for many years before it produces the fruit part we see.

Mushrooms grow from spores. A spore is similar to a seed but simpler in structure. When a spore is in contact with wood, and conditions are right, small thread-like strands grow from this spore, ultimately branching out into the wood. At the tip of each of these strands enzymes are produced which break down the tough wood cells, making their substances available to the mushroom for nutrition. This process continues until many tubes exist throughout an area of the wood. Collectively these strands are called the *mycelium.* This is the vegetative and main part of the mushroom, hidden within the wood, and even when exposed often too small to be seen except where mycelia are massed together.

The mycelium is the most important part of the mushroom, for it is the chief cause of decay in the forest, and without decay our forests would be impenetrable. Consider how long wood can last when protected from fungal decay: hundreds of years in many of our buildings and constructions. If there were no fungi in the woods, all the trees that had died and the leaves that had fallen during recent decades would still be piled on the earth as if they had just fallen. But with the mycelium of mushrooms constantly at work, all this forest debris is broken down into soil on the forest floor and made available to new growing plants.

After the mycelium has matured and conditions are right it produces a growth that pushes its way through an opening to the outside of the tree. The function of this growth is to produce spores, which will land on new trees and disseminate that species of mushroom. This growth is called the *sporophore*, a name meaning "the bearer of spores." Sporophores are what we see when we see mushrooms. The sporophores of bracket fungi usually produce billions to trillions of spores on their lower surface. The spores are microscopic but can be seen when thousands accumulate in one spot. The spores are produced on many types of structures and each type is characteristic of a certain *family* of mushrooms. Some are produced on the sides of gills, others in pores, others on a smooth surface, others in tubes or on teethlike projections. In any case, in bracket fungi and mushrooms in general, in order that the spores fall freely, the sporophore must be exactly perpendicular to the force of gravity; otherwise the spores stick to the gills, pores, etcetera, on which they are produced. Because of this, the living sporophores will continually orient themselves to be perpendicular to gravity if for some reason the log or tree they are on shifts position. This phenomenon can cause many interesting forms of sporophores. Frequently mushrooms start on a standing tree; the sporophores orient themselves in relation to gravity. When the tree falls, the sporophores are out of alignment and often grow new sporophores from the old ones, again perpendicular to gravity but obviously in different positions from the first and older ones. You could even take a tree with living sporophores and tilt it differently; come back in a month and see the changes.

All mushrooms are plants, but they are different from most other plants in one respect — they lack the green pigment, chlorophyll, that would enable them to make their own food with the sun's energy. In this sense they are more like us than most plants are; we can lie out in the sun for hours but we won't get any food or nourishment that way. We have to use the sun's energy indirectly by eating green plants or eating animals, which in turn have eaten green plants. Mushrooms are the same way; it makes no difference whether they are in sun or shade, they must be only where they can get the sun's energy indirectly, by living off other plants. Therefore, mushrooms are found only where there is organic material to live off. The more organic material, the better; this is why so many fungi are found in forests — on trees, on the fallen needles or leaves below, or on the roots.

For this reason a certain mushroom cannot grow forever on a log, for at some time it will use up the substances it can absorb. Sometimes Bracket Fungi are divided into two classes, depending on the parts of wood they dissolve for nourishment. One group, the White Rots, decompose most compounds of the wood, including the two major constituents of the cell walls, lignin and cellulose. They leave the wood white, spongy, and fibrous. The other group, Brown Rots, use only the cellulose of the wood cells, leaving the wood brown and crumbly. These two general types of rot are easily observed in the winter woods; check the rotted wood of trees and you will see that some is whitish, fibrous, and spongy, while other trees have dry, brown rotted wood, often breaking into small cubes.

Brown Rot is sometimes called "Dry Rot," but this is misleading, for no fungus can grow in absolutely dry conditions. For optimum growth, mushrooms need moist conditions and temperatures around 60 degrees, which explains why most mushrooms on trees grow in the fall. Many ground mushrooms also grow in fall, but they soon deteriorate, not having the leathery toughness of the Bracket Fungi.

Most of the Bracket Fungi are termed nonpoisonous, rather than edible, which means suitable for eating. In other words, they could be a survival food if necessary but are otherwise about as desirable as shoe leather.

Key to Winter Mushrooms

Common mushrooms growing on trees in winter can be divided into four categories depending on what they look like underneath. The four categories are listed below, and under each heading there are descriptions of common mushrooms you are likely to find. There are many others not included here, and some of the popular guides listed in the Bibliography may help you identify them if you decide you want to know more.

For most of these mushrooms there are no common

names; even their Latin names are continually changing as mycologists make revision after revision of groupings. The names used here are not the most recent classification but are nonetheless correct and represent a simpler grouping, one that I believe will be easier for the beginner to relate to.

MINUTE ROUND PORES COVER
THE SURFACE UNDERNEATH

— Top of mushroom is lacquered dark red, appearing shiny: *Ganoderma lucidum.*
— Growing only on White Birch; pores white or golden; thick lateral stem holds mushroom to tree; shaped like a piece of flattened bread dough: *Polyporus betulinus.*
— Smooth, concentric ridges on top; thick, hard as wood; white pores underneath, which show brown when scratched: *Ganoderma applanatum.*
— Hard as wood; concentric rings on top, each one lower than the next, older ones gray, newer ones biege; fine brown pores beneath; shaped like horse hoof: *Fomes fomentarius.*
— Brown pores; woody at base, thin at margin; showing a bright mustard brown inside when broken in half: *Polyporus gilvus.*
— White pores and white top; thin and papery; growing on dead Elm branches; sometimes shaped like little saucers: *Polyporus conchifer.*
— Light-colored pores; beautiful concentric zones of dark colors on top; downy hairs on top: *Polyporus versicolor.*
— Light-colored pores; concentric zones of different length hairs on top, some the length of velvet nap: *Polyporus hirsutus.*
Polyporus versicolor is similar but only finely downy; it is darker in color, and more common.

GILLS OR IRREGULARLY SHAPED
PORES UNDERNEATH

— White mushroom with large irregularly shaped pores; divisions between pores as thick as cardboard: *Daedalia quercina.*

— Concentric zones of gray hairs on top; creamy white gills beneath: *Lenzites betulinus.*

— Red-brown top with yellow margin; yellow-orange gills or irregularly shaped pores underneath: *Lenzites saepiaria.*

— Concentric lines of dull brown on hairless top; intricate design of mazelike pores or toothed gills beneath; paper-thin divisions between pores: *Daedalia confragosa.*

— White and downy on top; gray or lavender split gills underneath; small: *Schizophylum commune.*

HUNDREDS OF SMALL "TEETH"
PROJECTING DOWN UNDERNEATH

— Thin mushroom with faint concentric zones on top; small teeth beneath are lavender when fresh, turning golden brown with age: *Polyporus pergamenus.*

— White teeth projecting beneath, ¼ inch or more long; tends to grow in shelves along a branch: *Polyporus tulipiferae.*

MUSHROOMS THIN AND ABSOLUTELY
SMOOTH UNDERNEATH

— Projecting an inch or more from wood; concentric zones of beige on top; smooth beige surface underneath; wafer-like: *Stereum fasciatum.*

— Projecting less than a half-inch from wood; beige top

with some hairs; crinkled or extremely wavy margin: *Stereum gausapatum.*

Natural History Descriptions

Armillaria mellea

The vegetative portion of *Armillaria mellea* is commonly seen on trees that have lost their bark. It has a striking appearance and is included here to give another view of the biology of fungi. When the strands of the mycelium are

Rhizomorphs of Armillaria mellea

joined together into thicker strands they are called rhizomorphs. This is the case with *Armillaria mellea;* it has two types of rhizomorphs that are formed after the normal mycelium has lived in a decaying tree for some time. One type travels underground seeking out new hosts. The other type travels up the tree between the bark and sapwood. This kills the tree and the bark falls off and reveals the rhizomorphs: black tough strands of interlacing veins traveling up the tree. Their appearance has led some to call these mushrooms the "Bootstrap Fungi." When fresh, they are luminescent in the dark.

In fall the reproductive portion, or sporophore, of *Armillaria mellea* grows on the trunk or at the base of infected trees. It looks like a typical mushroom, and is quite edible. The fruit, not seen in winter, lasts only a week or so before rotting.

Cankers

Cankers are localized deformations of trees caused by fungi. These fungi are related to mushrooms, in the same group. The fungi enter the tree through wounds or broken branches, where spores land and send in the beginnings of the mycelium. In Cankers the fungi attack mostly the bark and the cambial layer of the tree. Usually the bark is just locally roughened or deformed, but sometimes it is killed and sloughed off, revealing the wood beneath.

Cankers are common on all parts of trees, especially trunks and branches. Some Cankers are annual and have a limited effect; others are perennial and can be more destructive.

Large canker on Oak

A common Canker on Cherry trees is called Black Knot. It usually first infects twigs, causing black, gnarled swellings along the twig. It can kill the twig in a year and in that time start to spread to the trunk. Lumbermen are aware of Black

Black Knot Canker

Knot, since when it infests trunks it makes the wood commercially useless. It is caused by a fungus named *Dibotryon morbosum.*

Some perennial Cankers grow only during seasons when the tree is not growing and stop when the tree grows. Because of this alternation, some trees can heal the area deformed by the Canker each year. This process can cause a series of concentric lines in the bark of the tree because of each year's cycle of growth and healing. These patterns are sometimes called Target Cankers.

Target Canker

Other Cankers can deform trees so much that they substantially weaken the trees; then, during windstorms or with snow load, the trees break at the cankered point.

Daedalia confragosa

The two common species of *Daedalia* are among our most beautiful winter mushrooms. Their beauty is mainly in the mazelike pores of their lower surface. The genus is named for this, referring to Daedalus, the Athenian architect of Greek mythology who built a labyrinth, or maze, for King Minos. The fruit bodies (sporophores) of these mushrooms

Daedalia confragosa

usually last only one year but may revive for another season. As they age, their lower surfaces change from a maze to a more gill-like construction.

Daedalia confragosa can occur in spectacular groups along logs or on branches. It is fairly thin, corky, and speckled light brown on top. When it is turned over you may find it partly gilled and partly mazelike, or all mazelike. The partitions underneath are thin as paper, presenting a delicate and intricate pattern, unlike the bold, thickly divided pattern of *Daedalia quercina.*

It is most often found on hardwoods, especially Willow, Yellow Birch, and Oak. It grows on only dead wood and is an important destroyer of slash timber that remains after lumbering. Its vegetative part causes a soft white rot of the wood, sometimes with zone lines at the outermost edge of its progress. The sporophores at times can completely encircle fallen branches or twigs.

Daedalia quercina

Daedalia quercina is heavier-set than its cousin *Daedalia confragosa.* Its mazelike pores are formed by thick dividers,

Daedalia quercina

more like cardboard than the papery divisions of *Daedalia confragosa.* Its underside pattern is therefore less intricate and more simple and bold. It is generally stark white when young, but it may turn to brown or black with age. The sporophore, being tough and corky, may persist for several years.

Its species name, *quercina,* means "of oak" for this is where it is generally found, although it can also occur on other hardwoods. It prefers large areas of wood such as logs, stumps, and trunks rather than branches or twigs. It grows all over the northern hemisphere.

Daedalia quercina causes a brown rot. In advanced stages of decay, the wood breaks into small cubical fragments, which can be crumbled between your fingers. Of the two species of *Daedalia*, this one seems to be the less common in the area of this guide.

Fomes fomentarius

Fomes fomentarius is distinctive, for it is shaped like a horse's hoof. The upper surface is crusty, in shades of light

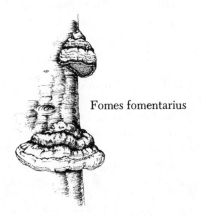

Fomes fomentarius

to dark gray, and composed of a series of concentric rings, each larger and lower than the previous one. A new ring is added during each favorable growing period. The under-surface is chocolate or rich brown, somewhat waxy, and covered with fine pores.

Fomes fomentarius rarely grows over six inches in diameter but, being common, is still easily seen on standing tree trunks. It is particularly obvious when it grows on the smooth bark of Beech, Birch, or Poplar trees, which it favors. Often several sporophores occur on a tree.

The spores of the mushroom probably enter the tree

Fomes fomentarius, *cut in half
to show annual layers of pores*

through broken limbs and wounds. Inside the tree, the root-
like mycelium forms straw-colored mats in the cracks of the
wood, attacking both the heartwood and sapwood of dead
or live trees.

Ganoderma applanatum

Ganoderma applanatum grows to be the largest of the
common winter fungi. It can grow to 2 feet in diameter, and
live for over fifty years. It has a flat upper surface, with
concentric rings showing as slight rounded ridges. The
upper surface is generally some shade of light beige or gray.
The lower surface, when the fungus is living, is white, but
scratch marks on it appear brown. Some people have

Top and underside of
Ganoderma applanatum

scratched whole drawings onto this mushroom's lower surface and have kept the fungus or sold it as a curio. Because this can be done, it is often called the Artist's Fungus. The sporophore can be as hard as wood and impossible to remove from a tree without tools.

Ganoderma applanatum is commonly found all across North America; it also exists in Europe. It produces a white

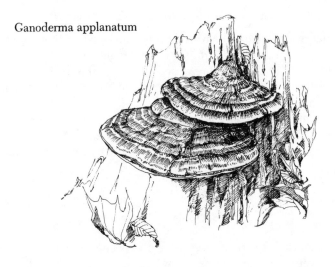

Ganoderma applanatum

rot that leaves the wood firm for a long time. It attacks both heartwood and sapwood and is found mostly on hardwoods although occasionally on conifers.

Ganoderma lucidum

Ganoderma lucidum has a dark, red-brown, shiny top, as if it were covered with varnish. The undersurface, at first white, may change to yellow-brown in color, depending on the age of the sporophore. Sometimes this species has a lateral stem, also a varnished red on top, holding the sporo-

Ganoderma lucidum

phore away from the tree. At other times when there are no stems, the fungi can grow so closely together, one above the other, that they become fused into one group. The upper surface is often very bumpy and wrinkled and always keeps its maroon lacquered quality.

Ganoderma lucidum is found mostly on stumps and at the bases of hardwood trees, often Silver Maple. Another very similar species, *Ganoderma tsugae*, grows only on Hemlock.

Lenzites betulina

Lenzites betulina is covered with concentric rings of gray velvety hairs on top and has large creamy white gills be-

Lenzites betulina

neath. The gills, though sometimes they run together irregularly at the margin, usually are separate. Its species name means "of Birch," but it is also found on other hardwoods and occasionally on conifers. The mycelium attacks mostly sapwood.

Lenzites saepiaria

Lenzites saepiaria is a lovely small yellow-brown mushroom seen mostly in early winter. It is usually found growing on conifers, and as you look closely at it you will find its under-

Lenzites saepiaria

side covered with small firm, plate-like gills. Its upper surface is plainer, with concentric zones of muted color variation and often with a pale yellow band at its margin.

Lenzites saepiaria is found all over the world and is an important destroyer of the discarded conifer logs and limbs left after lumbering. It also grows on processed lumber, such as railroad ties and building timbers. Its color, intricate lower surface, and small size make its discovery as exciting as finding a small jewel.

Polyporus betulinus

The species name *betulinus* ("of Birch") is the key to identifying this mushroom. *Polyporus betulinus* grows only on

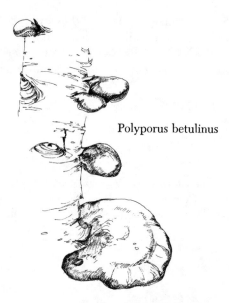

Polyporus betulinus

Birch, usually on White or Gray Birch. The sporophore looks like a thick puffed-up pancake on top. This upper surface is any shade from beige to white and it often has slight pits in the skin. The edges curl under and extend over the pores at the cap's rim.

The underside at first has white pores, which change to tan with age. The whole sporophore is spongy and moist when fresh, but dry and tough when old. Last year's sporophores are usually turned to dust by the quick work of insects. If you look closely, you will see that the sporophore

Polyporus betulinus *cut in half to show pore structure*

is growing out through the lenticels in the Birch bark. The vegetative mycelium attacks the sapwood and sends out sporophores wherever there is an opening. The mycelium causes a white rot, turning the interior of the tree into a spongy white mass of fibers.

Polyporus conchifer

Polyporus conchifer is a common sight in the city, for it attacks especially the dead branches of Elms. Since the Dutch elm disease started killing Elms, I am sure this mushroom has increased in abundance.

Large fertile sporophores and small sterile cups of Polyporus conchifer

Two types of sporophores are produced by *Polyporus conchifer*. One is shaped like a tiny dollhouse saucer and is sterile, not producing any spores. The other sporophore is fertile and shaped more like a thin rounded shelf. Both types are pure white, very thin, and dainty. Sometimes the fertile sporophore will grow around the cup-shaped sterile one.

This mushroom can occur also on Maple, Birch, and Cherry.

Polyporus gilvus

Polyporus gilvus is best identified by its color; it is mustard-yellow to brown throughout. When it is old, break it apart

Polyporus gilvus

and the mustard color will still be fresh inside. The young sporophore is fairly spongy, and the upper surface is rough, with little rounded bumps. It is about ½ inch thick at its

Back of Polyporus gilvus *where it was connected to the tree*

base and tapers to a thin margin. *Polyporus gilvus* causes a white rot in the sapwood of hardwood trees.

Polyporus hirsutus

Polyporus hirsutus is named for the dense small hairs that cover the sporophore's upper surface. Some other Polypores are also somewhat fuzzy, but once you find *Polyporus hirsutus* you will see how much longer the hairs on it are; they

Polyporus hirsutus

are about the length of velvet nap. The upper surface also shows concentric zones of gray, the hair in each zone slightly different in length from those in other zones. The bottom surface is porous and can be white, yellow, or light gray.

This is a common mushroom in winter; it occurs mostly on hardwood trees.

Polyporus pergamenus

Polyporus pergamenus is the most common winter mushroom in our area. On top it looks like many other Polypores,

Top and bottom of
Polyporus pergamenous

but underneath it has tiny pores which tend to elongate into toothlike forms; they are purple when living and tan or

Polyporus pergamenus

brown later. The small, thin sporophores usually occur in groups of fifty or more, and from a distance their tops look like white scales covering scars in dead wood. They often form in fire scars at the bases of trees. A common sight is the white tops of the sporophores covered with green algae at their bases.

Polyporus tulipiferae

Polyporus tulipiferae is distinguished from other Polypores by the long teeth or tubes, rather than pores, that make up its undersurface. The teeth are about as long as toothbrush bristles and are colored white to creamy yellow. The upper surface is also white, turning yellowish as it dries. *Polyporus tulipiferae* usually grows in long narrow shelves on fallen

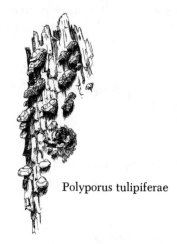

Polyporus tulipiferae

hardwood trees, and causes a white rot in the dead sapwood. It sometimes occurs on conifers. In winter it is an interesting study in black and white, appearing as irregular ribbons spreading across black stretches of fallen logs.

Polyporus versicolor

If you learn how to recognize *Polyporus versicolor* and *Polyporus pergamenus* you will know about 30 percent of the winter mushrooms you come in contact with. Of the

Polyporus versicolor

two, *Polyporus versicolor* is by far the more spectacular. On its upper surface are found beautiful concentric zones of tan, brown, gray, dark red, and dark green. Often the sporophores grow in whorls at the ends of logs, so that some have called them "Turkey Tails." The lower surface may be white, yellow, brownish, or light gray; it is uniformly covered with a thin layer of pores. Some people collect whorls

Polyporus versicolor *growing on Beaver-chewed tree stump*

of *Polyporus versicolor* for decorations around their houses; if you do this, be sure there are no insects in them or you will find little piles of white powder under each one in a few weeks. I once discovered an area long since chewed over by Beavers; on the top of each stump top were whorls of this lovely mushroom, as well as those of *Lenzites betulina*.

Schizophylum commune

Schizophylum commune is a small, fairly inconspicuous, mushroom, but it is common and easily identified when you turn it over. Its genus name, which means "split kind," refers to its unusual gills, which are small but neatly split down their centers. The gill surface is typically a very pale

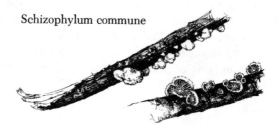

Schizophylum commune

blue when fresh. The upper surface is white frilled and covered with little tufts of cottony material. You will often find the sporophore on dead branches or on an old log that has attracted your attention because of other more conspicuous mushrooms.

Stereum fasciatum

Stereum is easily distinguished from all other mushrooms by its absolutely smooth underside, which shows no pores, gills,

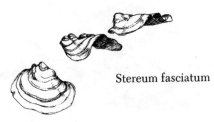

Stereum fasciatum

or teeth. *Stereum fasciatum* is a thin waferlike mushroom, with some concentric zones on its clay-colored upper surface; its lower surface is usually pale tan and absolutely smooth. Sometimes the sporophore is narrow at its base, at other times broadly attached. Nearby sporophores may be joined together along their sides.

This mushroom attacks both sapwood and heartwood of

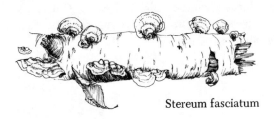

Stereum fasciatum

Oaks especially and is important as a decayer of slash wood left behind after lumbering. *Stereum fasciatum* is a common mushroom and resembles *Polyporus pergamenus* on top, but its poreless undersurface distinguishes it from the other fungus.

Stereum gausapatum

Stereum gausapatum is a small but common mushroom, especially on recently felled Oak. It is recognized by its ex-

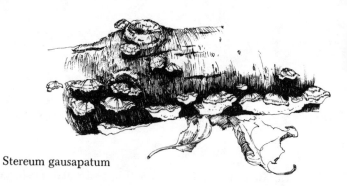

Stereum gausapatum

tremely wavy margin and lack of pores or gills underneath. It often grows in long ridges with the grain extending rarely more than ½ inch out from the wood surface. It may have matted hairs on its coppery, yellow-brown surface. The lower surface is often purple-brown and is absolutely smooth.

It produces a white localized decay of Oaks and is particularly successful at invading young sprouts that grow up around an infested older tree.

VII

Tracks in the Snow

*I*T IS HARD TO EQUAL THE EXCITEMENT of searching for the magical trails of animals imprinted in the snow's surface: the Fox's night wanderings, the Crow's landing in a field, or part of the Mink's circuit. To see an animal requires the gift of coincidence, you and it meeting at the same place at almost the same time. But the chances of meeting its tracks are much greater, for up to three or four days of its travels may be recorded, and you need to cross them at only one point.

More than just an impression in the snow, a trail is like a rope connecting disparate moments of time — both a record of the past and a connection to the present, for back on the trail are sketched the encounters of a living being, while ahead is the present animal continually leaving its life experience one step behind.

When looking at animals, we often miss the secrets of their private lives, since the animals have invariably seen us first and are reacting most to our presence. But the trail records the animal when it was alone in nature and brings us closer than ever before to its normal habits and perceptions of the world.

Besides the track itself, other signs should be looked for: stray feathers, a drop of blood, urine markings or a scat, twigs chewed, bark gnawed, kills stored, wood lodges, bank dens, tree dens, diggings in the ground, holes in the ice, torn-open hornets' nests, and countless others. Anything unusual in nature was affected by something or some one. What did it and why was it done?

Animal locomotion is extremely complex; the number of different ways four feet can move is astounding. But for the tracker it is valuable to be aware of at least the five basic modes of four-footed travel: two kinds of walking, plus trotting, bounding, and galloping. If you are limber there is no better way to understand these movements than by getting down on all fours and recreating them yourself, or watching someone else do it.

The simplest type of movement is the walk. In a walk a quadruped (four-footed animal) always keeps at least two feet on the ground. Doing this, it moves in one of two ways: either by moving both limbs on the right side, then both limbs on the left (pacing), or by moving hind left leg and front right leg, then hind right leg and front left leg (diagonal walking). Pacing makes the whole animal sway from side to side in a waddling gait. Diagonal walking is more balanced, since there is always support on both sides of the body. A child who has learned to crawl uses the diagonal walk of a quadruped.

Trotting can be similar to the diagonal walk, except that the whole body is lifted off the ground at one point. It is like the difference between our walking and jogging; in both, the feet alternate in the same way, but in the latter there is a moment between steps when the body is suspended in air.

In the fourth type of movement, bounding, the front feet reach out together and the hind feet follow as a pair, landing just behind the front feet or almost in the front prints. This movement is typical of members of the Weasel family.

The fifth common type of movement is galloping. It is

similar to bounding except that here the hind feet land to either side or ahead of the front feet. This is typical of Rabbits and Squirrels, and also all long-legged animals when they are trying to move fast. The human body is not made for this type of movement, and it's easy to pull a muscle trying to imitate it. If you ever have occasion to look further into animal locomotion, you will see how oversimplified this account is, but it is still valuable as a framework for interpreting tracks.

The ways in which most of even our common animals move has not yet been studied, and the effects these movements can have on track patterns is even less known. As you begin to notice the common patterns of tracks, musing over what type of locomotion created them can be a real challenge, especially in a number of the medium-speed patterns usually grouped under the term "loping."

I was once confronted with a particularly confusing track: a long trough 2 inches wide and 20 yards long. It began and ended abruptly with no sign of tunnels or further tracks. But, most curious of all, it proceeded directly through a fine wire-mesh fence with no sign of pausing or leaping over, as any animal larger than a mouse would have had to have done.

While puzzling over it I was momentarily distracted by a bird alighting on an electric line directly overhead. Suddenly it occurred to me — the electric line, the bird, the track! A wet snow had built up on the line and had been knocked off by the wind or a perching bird. From this anecdote it is clear that other things besides animals can make impressions in the snow. Blowing leaves or small cones form sketchy trails across meadows and frozen lakes; snow fallen from trees makes convincing prints beneath them, sometimes rolling as small snowballs down hills, leaving a clearly directed trail (surely they must be from an animal); and the drops from the snow melting off roof eaves mimic the trail of a scampering mouse.

So for especially mysterious prints always check above you for the possibility that bits of snow may have dropped from trees, telephone wires, or roof overhangs.

Good tracking conditions depend on the quality of the snow as it fell, the weather conditions after it fell, and the ways in which these two affect the movements of animals. Generally animals stay in dens or protected areas during bad storms and for a few hours after. They then come out only if it is their time of activity. So if a storm ends in the morning or middle of the night you will have to wait through one more night before the majority of tracks will be present, since most animals are active at night. Clearly, the longer the snow remains unmelted or undrifted after a storm, the more chances you will have to find tracks.

A dry drifty snow leaves few prints, and a wet snow will gather on branches and drop to the ground in the wind, leaving the forest floor pockmarked and impossible for tracking.

Tracks can be found anywhere, but they are often most common at the edges of habitats, such as where a forest and field meet, and particularly near water, as by lakes, along streams, or at the edges of swamps. When following a track, don't step into it, but walk alongside it; you may want to go back over it for measurements or photographs. Besides, a track is an exquisite, though fleeting, creation of nature, and others after you may want to enjoy it.

Key to Animal Tracks

When a track has been discovered there are two approaches to identifying it.

(1)   The first is to follow the trail until you find a clear print, one that shows the shape of the foot and number of toes. In this case, use the Key to Prints.

(2) If you cannot find a clear print, then you must use the pattern of the track for identification. In this case, use the Key to Patterns.

In most cases both methods are used, as well as knowledge of other signs and habits of the animal. Often tracks will not be clear in either pattern or print and you must use a range of knowledge to guess who the maker was. Reading through the natural history descriptions of the animals as well as becoming familiar with the keys will help you in these situations, and enable you to make at least an educated guess.

All the animals in our north can be divided into four groups based on the number of toes on their hind and front feet. Those in the first three categories have the same number of toes on each foot. In the last category, the animals have four toes on their front feet and five toes on their hind feet.

Measurements for length and width of prints are given. When both hind and forefeet are different, the distinctive one has been included and labeled. All measurements are merely guidelines, since print size varies with sex and age of animal and depth of snow. Prints are measured from one side of the toe pattern to the other, rather than by the general impression in the snow, which will invariably be larger.

Prints in each of the four groups are proportionately scaled.

TWO-TOED ANIMALS

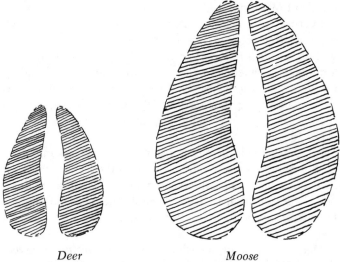

Deer
L. 3½ inches, W. 2½ inches

Moose
L. 7 inches, W. 5 inches

Often the front part of the toes is spread apart when the animal is supporting itself on soft surfaces. Also two small toes, called "dewclaws," may show in deep snow as two circular marks behind each foot.

FOUR-TOED ANIMALS

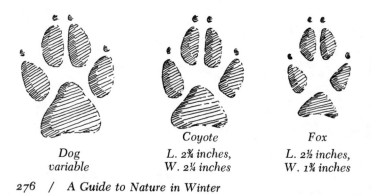

Dog
variable

Coyote
L. 2¾ inches,
W. 2¼ inches

Fox
L. 2½ inches,
W. 1¾ inches

All canines have four toes in an oval print with claws showing. All three are difficult to distinguish and one must rely most on other signs and the character of the trail. Read the natural history descriptions of Fox and Coyote, and see Key to Patterns.

Bobcat
L. 2 inches, W. 2 inches

Cat
L. 1 inch, W. 1 inch

Lynx
L. 3½ inches, W. 3½ inches

All felines have four toes in a circular print with no claws showing. Their prints are easy to distinguish by size alone. The Lynx has stiff hairs over its feet, which obscure its toe pads. Sometimes house cats are born with extra toes on one or more feet.

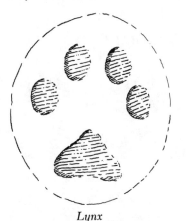

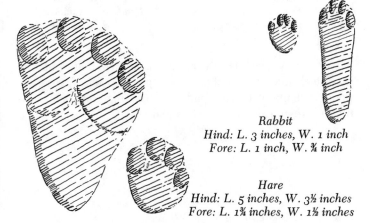

Rabbit
Hind: L. 3 inches, W. 1 inch
Fore: L. 1 inch, W. ¾ inch

Hare
Hind: L. 5 inches, W. 3½ inches
Fore: L. 1¾ inches, W. 1½ inches

The front feet of Rabbits or Hares could be confused with other prints, but their long hind feet and common galloping pattern distinguish them. The Hare print is particularly large and obvious. See Key to Patterns.

FIVE-TOED ANIMALS

Weasel
L. ¾ inch
W. ¾ inch

Skunk
L. 1¼ inches
W. 1 inch

Mink
L. 1¼ inches
W. 1¼ inches

Marten
L. 1¼ inches
W. 1½ inches

Fisher
L. 2½ inches
W. 2½ inches

Otter
Hind: W. 3½ inches
L. 4 inches

All of the Weasel family above have five toes, but the small fifth toe may not show in the print, in which case the pointed shape of the toe pad and claw together helps distinguish them from four-toed animals.

Raccoon	*Opossum*	*Muskrat*
Fore: L. 2½ inches	*Fore: L. 2 inches*	*Fore: L. 1½ inches*
W. 2½ inches	*W. 2 inches*	*W. 1½ inches*
Hind: L. 4 inches	*Hind: L. 3 inches*	*Hind: L. 3 inches*
W. 2¼ inches	*W. 1½ inches*	*W. 2 inches*

Raccoon prints have five clear toes on both hind and fore-feet, while Opossum prints show four toes and a thumb on hind foot, and those of a Muskrat show primarily four toes on a small front foot.

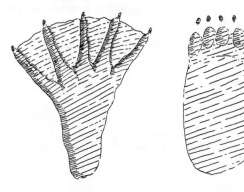

Beaver	*Porcupine*
Hind: L. 5 inches	*Hind: L. 5 inches*
W. 4½ inches	*W. 2½ inches*

The large-fingered and webbed hind foot of Beaver is distinctive. Toe pads of Porcupine rarely show up in prints, but the large oval print and the pattern of the trail are distinctive (see Key to Patterns).

ANIMALS WITH FOUR TOES ON FRONT FEET AND FIVE TOES ON HIND FEET

Mouse
L. ¼ inch
W. ¼ inch

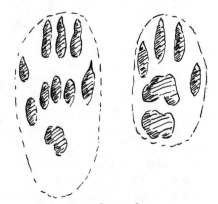

Squirrel
Fore: L. 1½ inches, W. 1 inch
Hind: L. 2 inches, W. 1 inch

See also five-toed animals: Muskrat and Opossum.

Key to Track Patterns

All animals can move in a variety of ways, but each also has a characteristic normal gait it uses most often. We can walk.

leap, or run, but we most often walk; a Rabbit can walk or gallop, but it almost always gallops. Our northern animals can be divided into four groups, based on their most common gaits and the patterns of tracks they create. Below is an outline of these four divisions, followed by a detailed discussion of each division and the animals within it.

Familiarize yourself with these basic patterns, so that when you find a track you can make a good guess as to which of four groups it belongs to; then use the detailed descriptions to make a more accurate identification.

FOUR BASIC TRACK PATTERNS

A.

A track that appears to be nearly a straight line of single prints is characteristic of all canines (Dog, Fox, Coyote), felines (Cat, Bobcat, Lynx), and ungulates (Deer and Moose). It is produced by walking or trotting — the most common gaits of these animals.

B.

Evenly spaced pairs or bunches of prints are the characteristic pattern of all members of the Weasel family except the slower-moving Skunk; this pattern includes the Weasel, Mink, Marten, Fisher, and Otter. It is created by bounding, a gait well suited to animals with short legs and long bodies.

When moving at slower speeds, they all tend to show the same variations; these are the faster gaits of the Skunk.

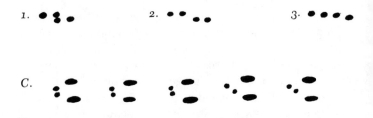

1.   2.   3.

C.

This pattern is a gallop, produced by the landing of the hind legs ahead of the front legs. It is the most common gait of the Rabbit, Hare, Squirrel, and Mouse.

Speeding up

Shrews and Voles are also included in this division, for they sometimes gallop; their tracks are best compared to those of the Mouse, since all three make very small tracks.

D.

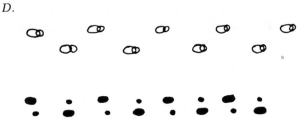

These are two types of walking created by wide, heavyset animals as they waddle along. This is the characteristic track of the Raccoon, Muskrat, Opossum, Porcupine, and Beaver.

Detailed Descriptions of Track Patterns

In each of the detailed sections is a chart, which shows what animals you can expect to find in the city, suburb, country, or wilderness. All identification relies on eliminating those choices which are unlikely, and these charts will help you do that.

Two measurements are often used in the descriptions: *stride* and *straddle*. Stride is the measurement from the center of one print or group of prints to the center of the next one in the trail. This is extremely variable, depending on the speed of the animal, and is listed here only as an average for the most common gait of each animal. When it is too variable, it is omitted.

Although stride is only of minimal importance for idenfication, straddle is very important and far less variable. Straddle is the width of the trail, and in cases of similar track patterns often is the key identifying factor. Nevertheless, it is still variable and only to be used as a guideline.

AA.

All two-toed, and most four-toed, animals make this pattern. When walking they place a hind foot directly in the print of the front foot. Sometimes the hind foot lands behind or to the side of the front foot, making these two variations:

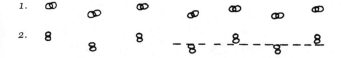

Notice that the paired prints in the second variation do not form a straight line like those of the Weasel family in pattern B, but are placed to either side of an imaginary line drawn down the center of the trail.

All of these animals display gallop patterns also, but they never gallop for very long in winter before changing back to more normal gaits.

What to expect where:

CITY	SUBURB	COUNTRY	WILDERNESS
Cat _____			
Dog _____			
	Fox _____		
	Deer _____		
		Coyote _____	
		Bobcat _____	
			Lynx _____
			Moose _____

CAT   Distinguished from others by small circular print (1 inch in diameter) and short stride. Average stride: 6–8 inches. Average straddle: 3 inches.

BOBCAT   Circular print twice as large as that of Cat, and found mostly in wilderness. Average stride: 10–14 inches. Average straddle: 4½ inches.

LYNX   Circular print almost twice as large as Bobcat's; toes seldom show through thick hairs on bottom of foot. Found only in Canada and northern border of United States. Average stride: 10–14 inches. Average straddle: 7 inches.

DOG   Dogs vary so in size that no generalizations of stride or straddle are useful. Oval shape distinguishes Dog prints from those of all Cats, but it is still easy to confuse Dog with Fox or Coyote. In general, their tracks show large feet, often being dragged, and their trail expresses a playful attitude toward their environment, rather than the keen awareness and stealth expressed in Fox and Coyote trails.

FOX   Straight lines of neat, oval prints, often following prominent aspects of the landscape: for example, a stone wall, the side of a woods road, a swamp edge, or a ridge. It expresses careful curiosity rather than the abandoned curiosity of a Dog. Travels long distances between hunting areas at a constant trot. Average stride: 12–15 inches. Average straddle: 3–4 inches.

COYOTE   Difficult to distinguish from Red Fox prints, for the size of the oval print and the length of the stride are similar. The straddle when walking or trotting tends to be larger. The prints are distinguished from those of the Dog by awareness and cunning expressed in the trail. Average stride: 12–15 inches. Average straddle: 4–6 inches.

DEER   Deer and Moose almost always leave some indication of their two-toed hoof at the base of their print. Since these animals are heavier than any of the canines or felines listed above and have thin, long legs, their feet penetrate the snow's crust and leave a deep wedge-shaped mark. Sometimes the foot drags between steps.

In deep snow other deer will follow in the same steps, forming even deeper wedges. Average stride: 14–16 inches. Average straddle: 6 inches.

MOOSE   Extremely large prints, sinking deep into the snow. Found only in Canada and northern border of United States. Average stride: 24 inches. Average straddle: 10 inches.

BB.

This pattern is created by both hind feet landing in the same spot as the front feet. Sometimes they land a little behind, creating separate bunches of three and four prints.

When the pattern forms pairs of prints, they are usually on a slight diagonal, rather than directly opposed.

What to expect where:

CITY	SUBURB	COUNTRY	WILDERNESS
Skunk _____
	Weasel _____
		Mink _____
		Otter _____
			Fisher _____
			Marten _____

SKUNK

A slow animal that leaves a meandering trail of small, round prints as it searches for hibernating insects, fruit, or small rodents. The skunk is included in this group because when moving faster it has the same variations of gait as the rest of the Weasel family does when moving more slowly.

1. 2.  3.

Skunk tracks always end at a ground den or similar lodging. Average straddle: 2½–3½ inches.

Note: Since all members of the Weasel family, except the Skunk, have similar patterns, you must use habits and size of straddle to distinguish between them.

WEASEL   The Weasel is the smallest of the Mustelids, but it varies most in size, since the Least Weasel is only half the size of the Long-tailed Weasel. Nevertheless, Weasel tracks and straddles are substantially smaller than those of the Mink, with whose track it might be confused. The Weasel often tunnels, stays away from directly entering water, and its body sometimes makes a connecting impression between prints. Average stride: 10–16 inches. Average straddle: 2 inches.

MINK   Mink hunts in and near water, and its straddle averages an inch larger than that of the Weasel. Weasel tracks can be minute, but Mink tracks are slightly larger than those of a House Cat. The only other Weasel family print near water would be that of the Otter, but the Otter's is over three times the size of the Mink's. Mink have large hunting circuits and frequently travel overland. Average stride: 18 inches. Average straddle: 3 inches.

MARTEN   Found only in Canada, and near the northern border of the United States — an unlikely print to find. The Marten lives in the forest and climbs trees as well as a Squirrel does. If a paired diagonal print leads to or from a tree, it may be that of a Marten. The Fisher also can climb trees but does not do so as frequently, and its print is almost twice as large. Mink and Marten could be difficult to distinguish except by habits, one entering water, the other climbing trees; but the Marten is so rare that in most areas it should not even be considered. Average stride: 24 inches. Average straddle: 3½–4 inches.

FISHER   The Fisher exists only in Canada and near the northern border of the United States. Its tracks are not rare in wilderness areas, and they are easily recognized by their large size. The tracks are often found in the mountains traveling cross-country. They could be confused with those of the Otter, since Otters also travel overland at times, but the Otter track is larger and the animal slides regularly in traveling. Average stride: 28 inches. Average straddle: 6 inches.

OTTER

Otter is the largest of the Weasel family and its track is easily recognized, since it slides with its body on the snow whenever doing so is easier than bounding. The slides are 8 to 10 inches wide and start and end with prints. Otters hunt primarily in water, but their tracks are so much larger than Mink's that there is no possibility of confusing the two. Otter tracks are not rare and may be found far from water. Average stride: 36 inches. Average straddle: 8–10 inches.

CC.

What to expect where:

CITY	SUBURB	COUNTRY	WILDERNESS

Squirrel ———————————————————————

Mouse ————————————————————————

      Shrew ————————————————————————

                  Vole ————————————

                  Rabbit————————————

                             Hare ————————

SQUIRREL   Squirrel tracks begin and end at trees and rarely differ from the gallop pattern. In deep snow the hind and fore print on each side make one impression, resulting in this track:

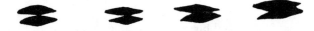

Squirrel tracks often lead to diggings in the snow where nuts were buried in the ground. The strides of Squirrels vary greatly but their straddles may be some clue to different species. Chipmunk — Straddle: 2–3 inches. Red Squirrel — Average straddle: 3–4 inches. Gray or Fox Squirrel — Average straddle: 4–5 inches.

MOUSE, VOLE, SHREW   These three types of animal make the smallest prints in winter. The Mouse typically gallops, sometimes leaving a tail drag.

It can leap long distances, and its track can be told from the Chipmunk's by having a straddle less than 2 inches and by the occasional tail drag.

Vole and Shrew also may gallop, but they usually run. The main distinction from Mouse tracks is that these tracks vary between galloping and different types of running.

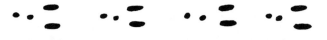

The two are distinguished from each other by the size of the straddle — the Shrew's is smaller. Mouse — Straddle: 1½–2 inches; mostly gallops. Vole — Straddle: 1½–2 inches; varying gait. Shrew — Straddle: less than 1½ inches; varying gait.

RABBIT, HARE

Rabbit and Hare always gallop, and tend to place their smaller front feet one behind the other, rather than paired like the Squirrel and Mouse.

Rabbit and Hare:

Squirrel and Mouse:

The hind feet of Rabbits and Hares are typically much larger than the front feet, and in the case of the Snowshoe Hare, they are so large that they are unmistakable (see Four-toed Prints). On the other hand, the Cottontail in shallow snow may show only the toes of its hind feet, making its trail look like the gallop of a House Cat.

In deep snow, the Cottontail may place both hind and front feet close together, making an impression where only its

body and tail show. Rabbit — Average straddle: 4–5 inches.
Hare — Average straddle: 7–8 inches.

DD.

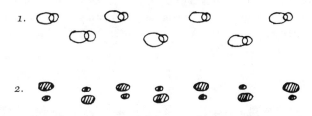

This pattern is seen only for heavyset, slow-moving, wide-straddled animals. All five of these animals spend a lot, or even the majority, of their time moving in other environments: the Beaver and Muskrat in water, and the Raccoon, Opossum, and Porcupine in trees. Hind feet are always larger, their print showing either on top of or overlapping with the front print (1, above), or alongside the smaller front print (2, above).

If these animals gallop, it will be for only short distances, and the spacing between gallops will be small, indicating a slow and lumbering movement.

What to expect where:

CITY	SUBURB	COUNTRY	WILDERNESS
Raccoon —————————————————————————————			
Muskrat —————————————————————			
Opossum —————————————			
Beaver —————————			
Porcupine ———			

RACCOON

Raccoon tends to place its larger hind foot beside the smaller front foot, as shown above. The pattern may be difficult to distinguish from the Opossum's, for the latter frequently walks with the same gait. But the Opossum trail sometimes has a tail-drag, while the Raccoon's never does. Details of hind prints easily distinguish the two (see Five-toed Prints). Average stride: 8–12 inches. Average straddle: 3½–5 inches.

MUSKRAT

Muskrats typically overlap their hind and fore prints and their tails may or may not make marks. Their prints are distinguished from those of the Raccoon by smaller front feet, occasional tail-drag, and by entering deep water or plunge holes. When the Muskrat is in its lumbering gallop, the tail mark shows irregularly between sets of prints.

The Muskrat, of course, does not climb trees as do the Raccoon and Opossum. Average stride: 3–4 inches. Average straddle: 3–4 inches.

OPOSSUM   Opossum gaits vary, making patterns similar to those of both Muskrat and Raccoon. Their stride is larger than that of the Muskrat and usually smaller than that of the Raccoon. Average stride: 6–8 inches. Average straddle: 4–5 inches.

BEAVER

The hind foot of the Beaver makes an impression that is easily recognized, even when obscured by melting. The large webbed area and narrow heel distinguish its prints from those of the other four animals in this category. A Beaver track will not be far from water, and the animal does not leave the safety of water except for a good reason, so look for evidence of gnawing nearby. Average stride: 4–6 inches. Average straddle: 6–8 inches.

PORCUPINE

Porcupines make a wide distinctive trough or series of prints. The prints are large and rounded, and they always alternate. Often arcs to either side show where the animal is lifting its feet around while waddling along. Its quilled tail usually drags over the trail, making a winding pattern over the prints. The trail usually ends at trees or dens before very long, at which point you may see evidence of chewed bark, or scats.

Many other animals will use a Porcupine trail also, since in deep snow it packs down a nice trough. Certain Porcupine trails between trees may be repeatedly used and worn down. Average stride: 5–6 inches. Average straddle: 8–10 inches.

Key to Bird Tracks

The tracks of birds are common and are often confused with those of other animals. Five prints are shown below. The first is a generalized print of all small or medium-sized birds that occasionally feed on the ground, such as Juncos, Sparrows, Starlings, Pigeons. The second is the Crow print, which is common and distinctive. The last three belong to our large ground-dwelling birds: Bobwhite, Grouse, and Pheasant. Note how all three have a short fourth toe.

Common bird print
L. 1½–2½ inches

Crow
L. 3 inches

Bobwhite
L. 2 inches

Grouse
L. 2 inches

Pheasant
L. 3 inches

Bobwhite and Pheasant are distinguished by the size of the print; Grouse is distinguished from the other two by the width of its toes.

Bird Track Patterns

Small birds either hop or walk. Their patterns are easily confused with those of Mice or Voles. Bird tracks, however, are longer and thinner and don't end at holes or trees, but just stop when the bird takes off. Wing marks in the snow are common and are a good clue.

Note how the hind toe drags when a small bird hops; this helps distinguish its track from those of Mice.

A small bird walking

A Crow walking from shallow to deep snow.

A Crow walks long distances in search of food, and in shallow snow its middle toe makes a drag mark.

In deep snow the Crow, Bobwhite, Grouse, and Pheasant all make a track similar to this.

The tail makes a mark as a bird lands, and its wings make a mark as it takes off.

Natural History Descriptions

Beaver (*Castor canadensis*)

Beaver tracks are rarely seen in winter, but evidence of the animal's presence will be abundant. Signs of Beavers include dams, lodges, ground dens, gnawed trees and wood chips, twigs and saplings stripped of bark, and water channels.

Beaver dams are infamous, as well as famous, as being some of the largest structures built by animals. Their function is to create an area of water that will provide the Beaver with safety and ease in transporting food and building materials. Although the Beaver is vulnerable on land, its main food, tree bark, exists on land. The pond allows the Beaver to reach its food source without ever being far from the safety of water. When Beavers eat away the food from around the dam, they either extend the pond by raising the dam or dig channels from the pond into good foraging areas. The pond also provides protection for the rest of the Beaver's activities, for the animal builds a lodge in the pond and is thus shielded by a moat from its predators.

Beaver with dam and lodge

The Beaver is not quite the master engineer it is made out to be. Dams are often built in difficult locations when only half as much effort might be needed to build one nearby. But once a Beaver chooses a location, it seems determined to make that location work. Shrubs are cut and placed trunk-end upstream in a line across the waterway. Rocks, mud, and branches are then piled on until the dam is sufficiently high and watertight. Dams may vary from a very few to 8 feet high. They are generally extremely sturdy and can be used by animals as bridges.

A Beaver lodge is made by piling up a mound of sticks and mud and then gnawing out a chamber inside. Beavers continually pack fresh mud on the outside but leave the top uncovered, possibly for ventilation within the lodge. Fresh mud is a sign that the lodge is actively used; in winter it will freeze up, making an impenetrable fortress at a time when predators can approach on the ice. Within the lodge, Beavers enjoy considerable warmth. A study in Canada showed the average minimum temperature of the air outdoors to be −30 degrees F. while average minimum temperatures inside the lodge were 34 degrees F.

The lodge usually has two underwater entrances, which

converge onto a feeding platform. A few inches higher and off to one side of this platform is a resting area covered with shredded wood (rather than grasses, which might rot).

Before winter the Beavers cut saplings and store them under the water near the lodge. In winter they leave the lodge and bring some of this food back to eat. Thus the Beaver rarely has occasion to leave the lodge or the protection of the pond in winter.

Beaver-felled trees are easy to recognize, for no other animals except humans cut trees. You may find felled trees at quite a distance from the dam or in an area where there are no dams, in which case the Beavers may live in bank dens similar to those of Muskrats or build their lodges in a river backwater. Beavers cut down trees for three reasons: to get food, to get construction materials, and to keep their teeth worn down. They do not eat the wood of the tree but only the young bark and so must cut down large trees to reach the young bark of the upper branches. These peeled branches are in turn used in the lodge and dam. Beavers cannot direct the fall of a tree they are cutting; their trees simply fall the way they are leaning. But even if a Beaver has enough food, it must chew, for its front incisors continually grow. If they are not worn down, they may grow so large that the animal won't be able to feed.

A lodge in winter may contain a number of Beavers. A pair tend to mate for life, and young Beavers stay with the adults for two years, so a winter family would contain two adults, two or more yearlings, and two or more kits born in the last spring. In the coming spring the yearlings are driven from the area and must start a life on their own.

Bobcat (*Lynx rufus*)

The Bobcat is the most common and widespread wild cat in North America. It ranges south into Mexico, and north into southern Canada.

Bobcat

As with most predators the Bobcat spends the majority of its time hunting. It is our only wild predator in the East that regularly kills Deer. This occurs mostly in winter, when the Deer are more vulnerable because of deep snow. Bobcats hunt at night and generally stalk Deer near the latter's bedding areas. Another of their methods of hunting is to lie waiting in areas where they know Deer will come, and then to bound onto them in a surprise attack. Bobcats kill Deer by attacking them on the back of the neck and biting through important veins. A Deer killed by a Bobcat is characteristically lying in the snow with its head bent back. There is often very little evidence of attack. The Deer is eaten, starting with the hind quarters; it is partly covered over with snow and debris when the cat leaves. Often a kill is used only for one meal, but the remainder provides important carrion for smaller predators, such as Foxes and Fishers, that would never attack a Deer themselves. Bobcats also regularly feed on smaller game such as Porcupines, Gray Squirrels, Cottontails, Rodents, and small birds.

The Bobcat is extremely wary of the snow. Although it is roughly the same size as the Lynx, the Bobcat has feet that are not as densely covered with hairs and so don't have as much surface area as those of the Lynx. In snow under 6 inches deep the Bobcat roams freely for distances of many miles a night. But if it encounters drifts or areas of snow deeper than 6 inches, it either avoids them or bounds through. When the whole snow cover is deep, a Bobcat restricts its movements, stays nearer to cached kills, and utilizes that food more. It rarely expends much energy chasing prey through snow; if prey is not caught within a few bounds it is given up.

The Bobcat beds down during the day. It beds under upturned stumps, in cavities among rocks, or on sunny knolls, depending on the weather. As it travels it explores all possible bedding sites within its range. Doing this serves the dual purpose of possibly finding prey in them and also being familiar with their locations so that the Bobcat can head for the nearest one after hunting.

Bobcats range over areas 25 miles or more in diameter, depending on the availability of prey. They mark their ranges with scats, urine, and scent excreted from scent glands. Although cats in general are believed to cover their feces, this is true only about 60 percent of the time with Bobcats, mostly younger cats doing so. Once a range is established by a Bobcat, other Bobcats seldom remain long within it but intrude only when passing through.

The track of the Bobcat is a larger version of the house cat track, being round, with four toe pads on each foot, and showing no claws. Cats use their claws for hunting, and retract them into their feet to keep the claws sharp. Canines kill mainly with their teeth, using their claws for traction and digging; their claws cannot be retracted and almost always show in prints. The trail of the Bobcat wanders considerably, as the animal explores all unusual objects and checks out all dens.

Cottontail (*Sylvilagus floridanus*)
Snowshoe Hare (*Lepus americanus*)

The winter habits and activities of Cottontails and Snowshoe Hares are easy to detect in the snow. Both animals eat

Cottontail with scats and chewed twigs

mainly the buds and twigs of sapling trees or shrubs in winter. These twigs are easily recognized, for they are cut at a neat 45 degree angle about 1 or 2 feet off the ground.

Rabbits also chew bark off the branches of Apple, Hawthorn, and other trees. Near where they feed there are often scats on the snow surface. These are slightly flattened spheres of chewed plant material, light brown in color; none of our other animals has a scat like this. Since the woody fibers these Rabbits eat in winter are hard to digest, such nutrition still exists in their scats. Therefore, when food is scarce, they may eat their own scats in order to absorb more of their nutritive value.

Rabbits and Hares forage at night and during the day often rest in "forms." Forms are small hollows among grasses and leaves, preferably under shrubs, where the snow is shallow, where there is protection from wind, and where the sun's warmth can penetrate the cover. In forms Rabbits rely on their ability to remain motionless and on the camou-

Snowshoe Hare

flage of their fur for protection. The Snowshoe Hare's winter coat is white, which makes it ideal protection in the Hare's northern range of constant winter snow. The Cottontail remains brown in winter, a color that is perfect for the patchy snow of its more southern range.

None of our Rabbits live permanently in underground dens or "warrens" as do European Rabbits; rather they build an above-ground nest of plant fibers when breeding and at other seasons use forms. Cottontail tracks may lead to the entrance of a woodchuck den or similar burrow, but the Rabbit is just remaining within the entrance. A Cottontail may even rest beneath soft snow and, when frightened, actually burrow through it.

Both animals keep to winter ranges of only a few acres, depending on the availability of food. In this range they reuse their trails so often that the snow can become packed along them. This familiarity with their range gives them an important advantage over their predators, which, generally having larger ranges, cannot know the nooks and crannies peculiar to smaller areas. The main winter predator of the Snowshoe Hare is the Lynx; for the Cottontail it is the Fox.

The Snowshoe Hare track is unmistakable from any other. It is only commonly seen in the northern states and Canada. A Squirrel track can resemble that of a Cottontail, but the fact that it sooner or later ends at a tree distinguishes it.

An unusual print of the Cottontail occurs in deep snow. Here it places hind and forefeet together, so that the whole body makes an oval impression, with a small mark at the back where the tail has hit the snow.

Coyote (*Canis latrans* variety)

The Coyote, which has always thrived in the West and Midwest, is now extending its range to the East. It is already present in the western sections of New England and

Coyotes with dead Deer

is believed to be expanding its range at about 15 miles per year. The Coyote of the East may be a new species from the western variety; it is slightly larger.

The reason for Coyote expansion is the extreme cunning and adaptability of these animals. They are able to live quite close to humans and still go unnoticed. They are feeding primarily on small rodents, carrion Deer, the unfinished prey of other predators, and fruits and berries. Often at the outskirts of cities they can find prey and carrion around dumps.

Their print is not much larger than the Red Fox's and indistinguishable from that of a small dog, except that it tends to be narrower than the print of the domestic dog. Like the Fox, it can best be distinguished from dogs by the keen awareness represented in its trail. It will approach points of interest cautiously, not making wasted movements, nor dragging its feet, and it will circle to smell the wind before bedding down for the day.

Coyotes often hunt the margins between two habitats and sometimes hunt in parallel pairs or loose groups of three or four. They move rapidly between known carcasses or favorite hunting areas, then slow down at those areas to search more intensively. Their ranges may be between 20 and 50 square miles in winter and may overlap with those of other Coyotes. They hunt open land most thoroughly and tend to avoid upland hardwood forests. Their trails often follow those of other animals, so as to conserve strength and avoid unaltered snow. Feral dogs (domestic dogs gone wild) are always an increasingly common animal of the woods, and their tracks and trails may be difficult to distinguish from those of the Coyote.

Coyote scats are larger than those of Fox but similarly pointed at the ends; they often contain much hair. Like other canines and cats, Coyotes place the scats at strategic locations within their territory. These "scent posts" may have scats of varying ages, possibly reflecting the frequency of the animal's visits.

Deer, White-tailed (*Odocoileus virginianus*)

To help them survive the winter, Deer stay within a limited area with which they become familiar, packing down a network of trails throughout it. The trails enable them to escape predators and get through deep snow to reach areas containing winter food. When these trails become particularly concentrated and the Deer remain in that location, it is

Deer rising from bedding area

termed a "yard," or "Deer yard." This is rarely a uniformly packed down area but rather a maze of small trails.

Where Deer stay in winter is mostly a function of the vegetation and topography. They generally bed during the day and feed at night. The bedding area must be warm, protected from sight, and not too far from food. In the South, this means on south-facing slopes, where they are protected from prevailing north winter winds and receive increased warmth from the hill's sloping toward the sun. In the North, they stay in Cedar swamps, which are generally lowlands protected from winds, or in Spruce groves, which also protect them from wind as well as from snow accumulation, since Spruces hold so much snow in their branches. In general, Deer try to take advantage of all the environmental factors they can to keep warm and conserve energy.

Winter food is a problem for Deer. Snow soon covers grasses except on south-sloping hills, where it may have melted, so most Deer switch to feeding on the buds of deciduous trees and the foliage of evergreens. They chew sapling trees down to nubs and eat the buds off all branches they can reach. Hemlock and Cedar needles are some of their favorites to browse. Deer-chewed twigs can be told from those chewed by Rabbits, for the Deer bite them off in their molars, making a ragged cut, whereas Rabbits use their sharp front teeth, making a neat 45-degree slice in the stem.

Most of the Deer's natural predators have long since disappeared from our area, so the Deer population is often too large for the winter food supply. As a result, many Deer starve or become too weak to defend themselves or manage in deep snow. But these dead Deer in turn are eaten by many of our smaller predators, such as Fox, Opossum, Coyote, Raccoon, Mink, and Fisher, which would not try to kill Deer themselves.

Two other signs of Deer are their beds and their scats. When Deer rest during the day or through a storm at night, they shelter the ground underneath them. You can frequently find these Deer beds as leafy areas surrounded by snow or as packed snow showing the outline of the resting Deer. Deer scats are distinctive, being dark black pellets each with a small point at one end. Their presence near the track, nibbled twigs, or a bedding area help make your identification positive.

When a Deer walks it places its hind foot directly in the print of its front foot; sometimes the footprints overlap slightly, making the print not quite clear. Patterns of White-tailed Deer movement are generally either walking, as described above, or galloping where the hind feet land ahead of the front feet.

Deer tracks may be of slightly different sizes, since does and yearlings are smaller than bucks. The front feet of Deer are larger than the hind feet, because they need to support the weight of the head and neck. Deer can spread the front parts of their hooves quite far apart when trying to support themselves on soft surfaces.

The track of the White-tailed Deer varies considerably, depending on the depth of the snow. In light snow, it is unmistakable, for the Deer is the only two-toed animal in this area, with a foot at most 3 inches long. The Moose also has a cloven hoof, but its feet are 5 to 7 inches long. As snow gets deeper, Deer's hooves sink all the way through, leaving a thin wedge-shaped impression slanting in the direction of travel.

Fisher (*Martes pennanti*)

The Fisher is a large member of the Weasel family. It is dark-furred, about the size of a Raccoon, although thinner, and has a long bushy tail. Its population and range have definitely been increasing over the last twenty-five years, so the chances of seeing the track or the animal are quite good now in the northern United States and Canada.

The best way to identify the print is to get a close view of the toe prints; there should be five, each with the mark of a

Fisher

claw. The print can be confused only with that of the Mink or Otter. Mink prints are much smaller and almost always neatly paired. Otters have larger tracks, with marks of webbed hind feet, and Otters frequently slide where the terrain allows. Both Otter and Mink enter water, but a Fisher will avoid it if possible. The Fisher's track, though sometimes paired, regularly shows a variety of patterns as the animal ranges freely across-country, from wooded mountainsides to lowland stream edges.

Fisher food is entirely different from that of the Mink or Otter. It eats Snowshoe Hare, Porcupine, Grouse, rodents, Raccoons, Deer carrion, and Shrews. It has a reputation for eating Porcupines, and studies show that Fishers do in fac feed on them, but Porcupines are only about 20 percent of a Fisher's diet. Carrion Deer are an important winter food, and Fishers will remain near a Deer carcass to feed on it for as long as it lasts. At other times Fishers are constantly moving on a circuit that may cover as much as 10 square miles. Fishers have been known to travel up to 15 miles in a single day. They are active during day or night and generally rest in caves or old dens.

Fox, Red (*Vulpes fulva*)
Gray (*Urocyon cinereoargenteus*)

Foxes are among the most exciting and accessible of all northern mammals to track.

Although secretive, they are common and prefer areas with both fields and woods, frequently making a habitat of suburbs and farmland. You are not likely to see evidence of a Fox in other seasons, but a thin layer of snow can boldly announce its presence.

What makes tracking Foxes most exciting is that you can see the mind of a predator in the wild. A Fox is always hunting in winter, and its kills and attempted kills are all

Red Fox walking from cache in foreground

revealed in its track. Since the Fox is seeking out other animals, following its trail will bring you in contact with other game also, so that you can spot their tracks and learn of the interaction.

Although Foxes hunt primarily at night, they may extend this activity into daytime during winter, since prey is harder to catch. They sleep in the open during the midday, curling up on the snow in some spot protected from wind but exposed to the sun, often on a slight rise of ground. They seldom sleep deeply but, more often, just doze off for a few seconds at a time.

A Fox must kill as much game as it can, for hunting conditions may be poor the next day. When game is available the Fox captures it; when it is not, the Fox can return to previous kills. Many kills are stored in caches: a pit is dug into the snow, the prey is placed in it, then covered over. Caches occur along the Fox's trail and appear as small areas of disturbed snow 6 to 12 inches across. Even old caches are repeatedly visited by a Fox, for they attract other animals that come to feed on the carrion, and the Fox may be able to catch them.

Another sign frequently seen along Fox trails is their scats or urine. These are odor communications to other Foxes and are usually placed at strategic points within a Fox's range. The scats are twisted, 2 to 3 inches long, and pointed at one or both ends; they usually contain hair or berries, unlike the scats of domestic dogs. Scats are often left at small physical landmarks, such as a break in a wall, a large rock, or a mound of earth. They may be of varying ages in a pile that shows that the Fox has repeatedly visited this spot. Like domestic dogs, Foxes leave urine markings along their trail. These may be used to help relocate a cache or may be to outline a territory.

Foxes tend to pair up in mid-December as a preliminary to breeding. From this time on, their trails may be seen in pairs, traveling parallel at one or two hundred yards apart or even following one another in the same prints. Mating occurs in January and February, and after this the two seek out and explore all dens in their range. Two or three are enlarged and cleaned out, but only one of these will be used. The Fox can dig its own den but more often will make over a Woodchuck den. The den openings can be obvious, for there is usually a large mound of excavated earth, there may be more than one entrance, and parts of prey animals may be scattered nearby. Den entrances average 10 inches wide and 15 inches high. Kits are born between mid-February and mid-March.

The home range of a mated Fox is about 1½ square miles; a solitary Fox may roam much farther. Ranges of Foxes sometimes overlap considerably, so that dens of different pairs could be quite close together.

Because the Fox often lives near humans, its tracks can be confused with those of the domestic dog. The best way to distinguish the two kinds of prints is to observe the overall pattern of the trail, for the realities of the two animals are totally different. A dog does not need to catch food, therefore it needn't be cautious, or alert to game; it can squander energy, romping through deep or shallow snow, and basically it has no enemies. The Fox is faced with the reality of winter survival; it must spot food and approach it carefully enough to catch it. It must always be on the alert for its prey and its enemies, and in winter it must conserve energy by walking in shallow snow, staying out of the wind, and getting the sun's warmth whenever possible.

The tracks vary accordingly. A dog track tends to be sloppy, often showing that the dog dragged its feet in the snow; a dog will explore, but without caution, and it will often gallop and romp without immediate purpose. A Fox track expresses extreme alert concern for every part of the animal's environment. The most common pattern is an almost straight line of neat prints. Objects explored are approached from downwind; galloping is used when the Fox is actually chasing prey. The Fox often walks along prominent aspects of the vegetation and topography — like following the woods' edge, or a stone wall, or a slight ridge. It has been generalized that a Fox's track is straight when the animal is traveling between areas, wandering when it is hunting, and circling when it is about to bed down.

Two species of Fox are present in northeastern and central North America: the Red Fox and the Gray Fox. The Red Fox is the larger and more common one, generally found closer to human activity. The Gray Fox is smaller, with a very delicate print, prefers more secluded areas, is able to climb trees, and frequently walks up fallen logs.

Lynx (*Lynx canadensis*)

The Lynx is strictly a northern cat and is not likely to be seen except in Canada and northern Maine. It is only a few inches larger than the Bobcat, but its feet are proportionately much larger. They are 3 to 4 inches in width and in winter are totally covered with hairs, which then help create a snow print 4½ to 5 inches in diameter. This print characteristically shows very little evidence of toe pads.

About 70 percent of the Lynx's diet in winter is the Snowshoe Hare; the rest is carrion and game birds. The Lynx and

Lynx

Snowshoe Hare seem to have a battle of snow adaptations going on, each developing larger feet, which support them more on the snow. The Lynx prefers to hunt from hunting beds, areas where it lies in wait for the Hares. When the population of Hares is great, the Lynx can do this more often; when Hares are scarce, it must travel more to find food.

A Lynx averages about one kill every other night. Although this figure remains constant for the Lynx, the distance it has to travel varies with the Hare population. Success in hunting is also intimately tied to the bearing strength of the snow cover: certain types of crust may support the Hare but not the Lynx; others may support neither or both.

The patterns of the track will be similar to those of dogs and cats — a straight line when walking or trotting, and a gallop when moving faster.

Marten (*Martes americana*)

The Marten is a relatively unknown mammal, which has become rare because of trapping. Of the tracks included in this guide, those of the Marten and Lynx are probably the ones least likely to be seen. Yet efforts are being made in Canada to preserve the Marten and enable it to increase. They have been partially successful, and so, with the hope that the Marten will increase its range, as has its cousin the Fisher, I have included it. Its track is not likely to be seen except in Canada and just into the northern edge of the United States.

The Marten is midway in size between the larger Fisher and smaller Mink. It displays track patterns typical of the Weasel family, but it is more arboreal than any of the other members, being as comfortable in trees as Squirrels are. It is one of the few predators on Squirrels, particularly the Red Squirrel, since the latter lives within the area of the Marten's distribution. Martens are also known to eat the Red-

Marten

backed Vole and Meadow Vole. The Marten hunts within a more restricted range than the Fisher and often intensively searches small areas of overlapping territory on successive days.

Obviously a track similar to but smaller than a Fisher's and one that ends or starts at a tree might be clues to a Marten.

Mink (*Mustela vison*)

Tracks of the Weasel Family can be difficult to distinguish. Weasel tracks are very small, Otter very large, but in between are the Mink, Marten, and Fisher. Each of these animals overlaps with the others in size, because females in each species are significantly smaller than the males. Therefore the way to identify them is to find which two or three animals your print fits in size and then to use habitat and habits to make the final estimation. Unfortunately the latter can also overlap.

The Mink, like its cousins the Weasel and Otter, is not a rare animal. It is widely distributed, and once you are away from cities and in good habitats, you have more than a good chance of spotting its tracks.

The animal is smaller and more common than the Marten, but larger than the Weasel. It will not climb trees like the Marten and it won't be found frequenting barns and fields in search of mice, as will Weasels. The Mink's favorite habitat is at the edge of lakes and streams, for its main food includes fish, crayfish, frogs, and Muskrats. In winter it feeds through a hole in the ice, digging into the mud to get the smaller hibernating animals. Larger prey, such as Muskrats, Cottontails, or Ducks, is often brought back to the den to be eaten or stored. Dens are situated near water, under

Mink

tree roots or in Muskrat or Beaver bank dens. The latter often have a few vertical entrances on land and one side entrance from water level. Females use dens more than males do and tend to stay closer to them.

Female Minks generally have a small range of between 20 and 50 acres, whereas males roam over areas up to 3 miles in diameter. Since Mink tend to circulate around their range, you may see the track only once and then not again for a couple of days. Similarly, not seeing it under good conditions does not mean that that area is out of the Mink's range; check a couple of times again. A female may traverse her territory in three days but a male may take over a week. During extreme cold weather, a Mink stays in a den and sleeps.

Moose (*Alces alces*)

The Moose is strictly a northern animal and except for northern New England and the upper Great Lakes region, it will only be found in Canada, unlike its relative the Deer, which is distributed throughout most of North America. Moose tracks are similar to those of the Deer, but they are twice as large, so there is little chance to confuse the two.

Moose

The cow Moose keeps her calf with her through its first winter, and its track may be as small as that of a large buck Deer, but in this case you are sure to see the cow Moose's track nearby.

The bull Moose have their "rutting" season in fall, when they compete for dominance. They grow extremely large antlers for this competition, but shed them by January. The cows generally keep the bulls away from their calves in winter.

Moose in winter feed primarily on the buds and bark of deciduous trees and the foliage of evergreens. Their favorite foods in the East are Balsam Fir, Hemlock, Willow, White Cedar, Aspen, and Alder. They frequent lowland creek bottoms and evergreen forests, gathering there in small, loose groups. Their grouping is not used, as in the case of Deer, to trample down important paths; it is merely a function of availability of food. Moose seem to have little trouble coping with most snow conditions, since their long legs lift their chests above the snow. Even up to 30 inches of snow gives them no problem.

The Moose's main predator in winter is the Wolf. There are two reasons for this: smaller mammals, the Wolf's summer prey, are covered by snow, and the Moose's summer defense, swimming into water, is not possible. Packs of Wolves may surround a Moose and slowly harass it to death.

Mouse (*Peromyscus* species, *Mus musculus*)

"Mouse" is a name used in referring to a large group of similar small rodents. They have large ears and eyes, long tails, generally pointed faces, and they live above ground. All these characteristics distinguish them from the other large group of small rodents, called Voles, which have small ears and eyes, short tails, blunt faces, and which generally live in tunnels under grasses and leaf litter.

The three most common Mice in eastern North America

are: two native Mice, the Deermouse and the White-footed Mouse, and an introduced Mouse, the House Mouse. All three types may be found in human habitations but only our native mice readily survive in the wilds. Their main food is seeds and nuts but when they are living in buildings, they will eat any scraps.

Mice are considered strictly nocturnal but in the wild will feed in broad daylight. Mice eat all kinds of food: berries, buds, bark, nuts, seeds, greens, insects, and even carrion if it is available. They also prodigiously store food in a number of areas within their territory, such as under logs or among rock crevices. Their territories are rarely more than a quarter-mile in diameter, but their trails will often be longer, as they frequently explore all over their territory, checking out every small hollow and burrow.

Mice have an amazing ability to leap and climb, which enables them to get to many spots that you would think they could never reach. Because of this agility, they can nest just about anywhere. A Mouse nest is composed of some soft material gathered together into a mass, within which the Mice create a small chamber. Often more than one Mouse lives in a nest, and since they leave their scats within the nest, it soon becomes fouled; at that point they move out and make a new one. Nests can be found within walls, in logs or stumps, beneath tree roots, or even in birds' nests. As a matter of fact, it is quite common for Mice to use birds' nests for homes, so when you see a birds' nest that seems particularly bulky, carefully open it apart. You may find three or four mice huddled together in a Cattail down lining. Some Mice also nest in old Woodpecker or Chickadee treehole nests; they have been found as high as 50 feet up in the trees.

Mouse tracks can be found anywhere, especially around barns, swamps, and field edges, and in woodlands. The most common gait of a Mouse is galloping, the hind feet landing ahead of the forefeet, forming a miniature track similar in pattern to that of a Rabbit or Squirrel. During warm spells, Chipmunks emerge onto the snow, forming a similar pat-

Deermouse with nest in background

tern, except that their straddle is greater than 2 inches whereas the straddle of Mice is less than 2 inches.

Two other tracks of similar size are those of the Shrew and Vole. Because these animals live mainly in tunnels, their characteristic track is running rather than galloping, but they may also gallop. The clue is to follow the trail: if it continually gallops it is probably a Mouse; if it varies a lot or is not a gallop it is probably a Shrew or Vole.

Muskrat (*Ondatra zibethica*)

Muskrats are fairly well prepared for winter in their water environment, so they may not even show their tracks on land, but if they do, it will always be near a source of water, whether it be a lake, swamp, stream, or road ditch. They feed in winter primarily on rootstocks of water plants such as Cattail or Arrowhead. They also eat crayfish, snails, freshwater clams, and some fish. If an orchard is especially close, they will roam on land for the fallen fruit, but generally they stay right near the water, for they are slow on land and vulnerable to a variety of predators.

Muskrats build two types of homes, one of which is particularly evident in winter: a lodge shaped like a miniature Beaver lodge and made of Cattails, mud, and small water plants. The Muskrat builds up the mound of plant material and mud and then, like the Beaver, eats and digs out an entrance from underwater and a chamber inside. The area inside is linear, with a number of enlarged spaces for sleeping, depending on how many Muskrats stay in the lodge. The lodges may be up to 4 feet in height and 8 feet in diameter, but are generally smaller. Water birds sometimes build nests on top of them, water snakes may bask on them and hibernate in their walls, and Snapping Turtles sometimes lay their eggs inside abandoned ones.

Muskrat with snow-covered home in background

The other home Muskrats make is in the bank of a lake or stream. They dig an underwater entrance and then an enlarged chamber above water level. Sometimes there are other entrances directly down through the ground above the chamber. These are called "plunge holes" and are used for quick escape from danger when foraging on land. Bank homes are sometimes taken over by Mink, or enlarged and used by Beavers.

Muskrats that live in swampy areas often excavate extensive channel systems radiating from their lodges or burrows; when water is low, these remain filled and provide protection as the animal feeds. Sometimes these are dry in winter, and the Muskrat's tracks will show in them.

The tracks are quite small, and often will show where the tail dragged, although it can also be held above the snow. Typically a Muskrat puts its hind foot close to where its front foot went, but variations in this pattern will be seen. In its running gait, the hind feet land ahead of the front feet in a pattern similar to the gallop of many animals. The Muskrat's long toe prints could be confused only with those of the Raccoon or Opossum. The Raccoon's prints, however, are easily distinguished, for they are almost twice as large. Those of the Opossum can be distinguished by also being larger, by having an opposable thumb at a weird angle, by ending at trees, since the Opossum regularly climbs, and by not entering into plunge holes or deep water.

Opossum (*Didelphis marsupialis*)

The Opossum is slowly extending its range to the north even though its body is ill suited for the cold. Its ears and tail are hairless and very often bits of them freeze and break off. Nevertheless, some force is pushing them north, and they are surviving.

Opossums regularly climb trees, and their opposable thumb, as well as their tail, which can support them from branches, undoubtedly helps them. They eat fruit and ber-

Opossums

ries off trees, also feed on small mammals, insects, reptiles, and amphibians.

Opossums stay in dens for most of the winter, usually as lone individuals. They readily use the network of dens also used by Raccoons and Skunks, though rarely at the same time. Tree dens and building foundations are also used for daytime resting areas. They come out to feed mostly at night and their home range may be up to 50 acres.

Otter (*Lutra canadensis*)

Otter tracks are usually found at the spillways of lakes where fish gather, or along sections of streams too shallow for the Otter to swim in. It prefers water habitats, for its diet is primarily fish, crayfish, turtles, and frogs. But Otters also frequently travel overland to hunt small rodents, and move to other areas of water for fishing. They may travel up to 3 miles overland in search of food or new waterways.

Their track is unmistakable, for they have adapted to snow travel by combining bounding and sliding. They typically take two to four bounds and then slide 5 to 15 feet. The slide is wide and looks as if someone had pulled a toy toboggan over the snow; it starts and terminates with a group of prints. Otters usually slide down slopes, and also when going up a slight incline, they may slide by pushing with their hind feet.

An emphasis on the playful character of the Otter is misleading. The fact that animals raised in captivity are playful with humans is also true of Mice, Squirrels, Skunks, and Raccoons, among others; and Otters' repetitive use of a single slide is the exception in nature. A more realistic look has shown that they prefer to walk down slopes into water and that sliding in snow is an important adaptation to the restrictions of snow travel, enabling the animal to forage on land in times of winter food scarcity.

When fishing in winter, the Otters keep a hole or two

Otters

open in frozen lakes. They dive into the water, chase the slower fish in toward shore, where they catch them in their mouths; they emerge from the water and eat the fish nearby.

Otters use dens for winter protection; these may be up to 500 feet from water, in a Woodchuck burrow, or under upturned tree roofs. But more often they are in the bank of the stream or lake — underground burrows that are frequently old bank dens of Muskrats or Beavers.

Porcupine (*Erethizon dorsatum*)

It is hard to follow a Porcupine track for more than a quarter-mile without coming upon some sign of the animal's activities, for Porcupines are relatively sedentary creatures and find it hard to walk in deep snow. The tracks are distinctive in themselves and in combination with evidence of the animal's activity are unmistakable.

Three signs of the Porcupine's activity are easily spotted: its tree or cave den, its scats, and evidence of its feeding. Often you will find the animal's tracks leading to a den among rocks or a hole in a tree. If these homes have been at all used by a Porcupine they will have the animal's scats covering the floor, for Porcupines defecate in their dens all the time and don't seem to mind the filth or stench. They seem to use the den until it is so filled with scats that there is no room left for them. The scats are distinctive: they are oval, mustard-brown, composed of wood fiber, and have a somewhat sweet smell.

If a Porcupine is not in its den it will be in a tree feeding. Porcupines eat the inner bark primarily, and favor coniferous trees. Their chewing is easily distinguished from that of Beavers, both because it occurs high on the tree and because it never penetrates the wood. A few scats may be present at the base of a feeding tree. A common habit of Porcupines is to chew the tips off Hemlock branches, discarding the last foot of the branch on the ground. An area

Porcupines

of snow covered with these pruned branch tips is a sure sign of Porcupine; this litter also aids White-tailed Deer, providing them with winter browse they could otherwise never reach.

In the case of the Porcupine, evidence of its presence is more common than sight of the animal itself. But if you find either fresh scats or tracks, and then look hard in the tops of feeding trees you may spot it. It is often less conspicuous than you might think.

If snow cover is 6 inches or more, Porcupines must plow through the snow, forming a trough about 8 inches wide. The prints alternate and are slightly pigeon-toed. The trail usually ends at a den or a foraging tree.

Raccoon (*Procyon lotor*)

Raccoon tracks are likely to be found at the edges of cities as well as in the country, for Raccoons are opportunists, able to take advantage of human refuse by raiding backyard trashcans and staying near town dumps. Being omnivores, they eat whatever is available, but in the wild they prefer nuts and berries, eat frogs, clams, snails and crayfish along streams, and an occasional bird or small rodent.

Raccoons are not as active in winter as they are in other seasons. They build up some fat reserves in fall which enable them to stay holed up in their dens during deep snow or very cold weather.

In some areas Raccoons, along with Opossums and Skunks, may use a number of particularly good dens over the year. All of these animals have similar intermittent periods of activity during winter. Many of them frequently switch dens after a night's ramblings. Because they do this, they all get to know the best dens over an area of many hundred acres, and one den may be inhabited by Skunk one night and Raccoons the next. Skunks tend to use ground dens, Opossums tree dens, while Raccoons use both. By

Raccoons

following trails you may be able to locate dens, but since the animals can wander over a mile at night you may have to follow them for quite a distance. Since these three animals may use an area for several generations, sharing dens and eating similar foods, trails become worn in the forest and can be seen as a winding impression even with autumn leaves on the ground. When snow falls, the prints of one or more of these animals will be along the trails.

Raccoons often spend the warmer days of winter resting high in the branches of trees. Tracks that lead to a tree may help you to spot the animal; Raccoons may not rest in the same tree on two consecutive days. Frequently their scats can be seen at the bases of trees they have climbed. The scats are about ¾ inch in diameter and have flat ends; they are crumbly and often contain bits of insect or crayfish shells and, possibly, hair.

Raccoon tracks are distinctive. They have five clear long

toes on each foot, and the long hind foot comes to a blunt point at its heel. Claws may or may not show. The pattern is typically in pairs, one hind foot next to one forefoot. This may represent a style of movement called "pacing," where both left feet are moved, then both right feet. Raccoons often walk on fallen logs or travel along the edges of streams and wet areas.

Raccoons tend to feed in small groups at night, and being part of a group gives a Raccoon dominance over solitary individuals. When one group is feeding in an area, they may keep a solitary Raccoon away or, if another group approaches, allow them to stay after appropriate signs of dominance or subordination have been exchanged.

Shrew (Family *Soricidae*)

Shrews are the smallest and most common mammal in North America, inhabiting almost every country habitat,

Shrew

from fields to woods to swamps. But for all this they are rarely seen, for they live just under the soil surface, sharing with Moles and Voles a network of tunnels and nests.

Shrews eat insects, earthworms, nuts, and berries, and occasionally kill small Mice or other Shrews. To gather these foods they travel in both surface and subterranean tunnels. A Shrew's own underground tunnel has a short vertical section of a few inches, then may travel horizontally for a few feet. But these tunnels are probably more for protection than feeding, since the tunnels of Voles and Moles are readily available.

Shrews are active only for short periods at anytime, day or night. The rest of the time they sleep in their tunnels, sometimes huddled together for warmth. Their eyesight and sense of smell are poor, but their hearing is well developed and probably relied on for protection in the wild. There are many species of Shrews, of varying sizes and habits. Those that live in swamps even readily take to water and may be seen swimming.

In winter, Shrews often tunnel through the snow. Their tunnels are about 1 inch in diameter and frequently come to the surface at a tuft of grass or the base of a shrub. It may be that the snow is softer at these points, so that the Shrew can penetrate surface crusts. The Shrew's track shows a variable running gait with a straddle about an inch wide, never more than 1½ inches. This straddle size distinguishes it from the Vole's track, which is similar in its evidence of variable running gaits but which shows a straddle of 1½ inches or greater. The Vole's tail will not show in the track, but the Shrew's will leave a mark about 50 percent of the time.

Skunk, Striped (*Mephitis mephitis*)

The Striped Skunk is active in early and late winter, but during midwinter is more or less dormant. Skunks prefer

Striped Skunk

areas of mixed woodlands and fields; their winter food consists of fruit (apples, shrub berries), small mice, shrews, carrion, garbage, nuts, seeds, and grains. This winter diet is in marked contrast to its largely insectivorous habits of spring, summer, and fall.

Skunks spend most of winter holed up in underground dens. The dens are often old Woodchuck, Squirrel, or Badger homes refilled with new grasses and dried leaves and stoppered with a plug of similar material. Up to twelve Skunks may be in a single den, usually with many more females than males; this proportion has led some to believe that they are polygamous. The dens are frequently on the sides of hills, where drainage is best, or along fencerows, where farm equipment won't damage them. Skunks can be found from the wilderness right on into the edge of the center city.

Skunks are members of the Mustelids or Weasel family, which includes Mink, Otter, Marten, Fisher, and Wolverine. But they are nowhere near as speedy as their relatives and prefer to wander slowly across the land, eating more vegetable matter and using scent rather than speed for defense. The Striped Skunk will spray only as a last resort. First, it will try to gallop away, then if that fails, it will turn to face you while stamping its front feet. If this does not make you retreat, it will turn and spray its scent. It can spray up to 8 feet away, usually in an arc so as to be sure to hit its target.

Striped Skunks come out to forage only at night. As yet there is no conclusive evidence that weather determines their activities. It is also unclear how far they may forage. Some people have followed Skunk tracks up to 3 miles long; most are much shorter, and it is believed that females range less far from the den than males do. A foraging Skunk will check most dens it comes across and may switch dens a number of times during the winter. The dens it uses may be used at other times by Opossums and Raccoons.

The track is usually seen coming from a den, where the fresh earth from inside will darken the snow at the entrance. As Skunks look for food they wander here and there, the foot pattern varying tremendously. It is this meandering trail of varying prints that is often a good clue to the Skunk. Its track varies with increasing speed, forming patterns similar to those formed by the medium gaits of other members of the Weasel family.

Squirrel (Family *Sciuridae*)

Squirrels, because they are adapted to many environments, including the city, are some of the most successful animals in North America. In the West and Midwest most Squirrels, chiefly ground-dwellers, hibernate through winter. In the north central and northeastern regions most Squirrels are tree Squirrels; they are active all winter. These include the Fox Squirrel, *Sciurus niger,* in the central United States, the Gray Squirrel, *Sciurus carolinensis,* in the eastern United States, and the Red Squirrel, *Tamiasciurus hudsonicus,* in Canada and the northern United States.

The Red Squirrel is the smallest of the three and, unlike the other two, is almost always associated with coniferous trees. It stores cones and nuts in large caches under tree roots or in underground burrows. Near these caches are

Gray Squirrel

often piles of discarded shells or scales chewed off Pine or Spruce cones. These piles, called "middens," are a clue to its presence. The Red Squirrel also tunnels through snow to search for nuts on the ground or to have safe and easy access to a shrub or tree that has fruits. The tunnels measure 2½ inches in diameter and have double grooves in their floors, caused by the Squirrels' running. They can be up to 100 feet long.

Red Squirrels make leafy nests in the treetops and often line them with Red Cedar bark as insulation. If you find Cedars stripped of their bark, you can guess that a Squirrel's nest is nearby. Red Squirrels will also live in tree dens or dens underneath the ground. A single Squirrel may have all three of these types of home. The range of a Red Squirrel is small, rarely more than 400 feet in diameter.

Unlike Red Squirrels, Gray Squirrels and Fox Squirrels bury nuts and other food, each piece separately, in the ground. They dig a small pit, place the food in it and tamp it down. In winter they go to the areas where nuts were cached and rely on smell to locate them. One attempt to check their ability to do this found that out of 250 nuts stored, only two were uneaten by spring and one of those was rotted.

Gray and Fox Squirrels, like Red Squirrels, live in tree dens or leaf nests. When using tree dens, they often seek out old Flicker homes or places where a limb has broken off and the wood rotted out. Squirrels sometimes gnaw back the bark to enlarge the entrance — seeing evidence of this may help you decide if a tree den is in use. Gray and Fox Squirrels invariably line their tree dens with leaves and plant material.

The Gray Squirrel lives in Oak or Beech woods, and its range may be up to 7 acres, depending on food availability. The Fox Squirrel is more apt to live in woods mixed with farmland. It spends more time on the ground than the other two and often nests in lone trees out in fields.

In December and January, male squirrels get more aggressive toward each other and start to chase females through the trees as a preliminary act to breeding. Young are born in March, at which time the female becomes fiercely protective of her young and keeps the male away.

Squirrels move on land very much like rabbits, their larger hind feet landing ahead of their forefeet, except that with Squirrels the front feet are usually paired, whereas Rabbits' are placed one behind the other. Squirrel tracks can also be distinguished from those of Rabbits by the fact that they start and end at trees. Squirrel prints are also distinctive: when visible, they show small delicate toe pads — four on front feet and five on hind feet. Rabbits show four furry pads on all feet.

The Eastern Chipmunk, *Tamias striatus*, although dormant through most of winter, occasionally comes onto the snow surface. Chipmunk tracks are slightly smaller than the Red Squirrel's and larger than the Deer Mouse's. The track of the Flying Squirrel, *Glaucomus* species, is also occasionally seen. The animal is nocturnal and doesn't often land on the snow, since it glides between trees. But when it bounds through snow, its prints are connected on either side with lines where the large flaps of skin used for gliding leave their imprint.

Vole, Meadow (*Microtus pennsylvanicus*)
Redback (*Clethrionomys gapperi*)

Voles and Mice are the smallest members of the Rodent family. Voles differ from Mice by having small ears and eyes, blunt profiles, and short tails, and by living in tunnels under leaf litter or within meadow grasses. They are the most important source of food for our birds of prey and many carnivorous mammals. Ninety-five percent of our eastern Hawks' and Owls' winter food consists of the Meadow Vole, *Microtus pennsylvanicus*, and to the North and West the Boreal Red-backed Vole, *Clethrionomys gapperi*, is equally important. Both animals are prolific and

Meadow Vole with tunnels

create an essential link in the food chain between grasses and carnivores.

Because Voles move mostly in tunnels, their tracks are not commonly seen. But as the snow melts their tunnel network in the lower level of the snow cover becomes obvious; the tops of the tunnels melt first and expose rows of tracks worn down inside. Sometimes Voles dig holes from under the snow to the surface for ventilation among their subnivean burrows. When their tracks are seen, they can be recognized by evidence of varying gait, changing even over short distances; Voles tend to run rather than to gallop. The tracks are distinguished from those of Shrews by having a straddle greater than 1½ inches and from those of Mice by the fact that they don't show a tail mark or evidence of consistent galloping.

Most Meadow Voles live in meadows, while the Boreal Red-backed Vole lives in woods; both prefer moist areas, and their tracks can often be found near marshes. A common habit for them in winter when food is scarce is to gnaw the bark off shrubs and fruit trees. At the base of these trees or shrubs you may find sections stripped of bark and with many tiny indentations from the animal's two front teeth.

Voles make nests among the grasses; these are woven bits of rootlets and grass fiber formed into a spherical nest with a chamber inside. Unlike Mice, they do not leave their droppings in the nest but deposit them in piles at crossroads in the tunnel network. These can be found by lifting the grasses from over the tunnels until you come to a large intersection.

Weasel (*Mustela* species)

The Weasel is adapted primarily to catching Mice. Its small head and sleek body enable it to enter Mouse runways and Vole tunnels. About 75 percent of its diet is small rodents; the larger Weasels also eat Rabbits, Squirrels, Rats, and Shrews. Because of their food preferences, the tracks of Weasels are frequently seen near barns and sheds, where mice spend the winter. Weasels seem to be distributed fairly evenly over the country, in woods, fields, around farms, and at the edges of cities. In winter they live in dens, which may be underground, in woodpiles, or under buildings. Weasels are active at night and characteristically hunt by smell, zigzagging over the snow in search of a scent. When they locate prey they chase or burrow after it. Weasels kill by biting through the back of their prey at the base of the skull. They are scrappy fighters and can capture animals much larger than themselves. They rarely feed on carrion.

Weasels are the smallest member of Mustelidae, the Weasel family. The Least Weasel, *Mustela rixosa*, measures a mere 5 to 6 inches in length, while the largest, the Long-tailed Weasel, *Mustela frenata*, is still only 10 inches long (neither measurement includes the tail). Their size is important in distinguishing their tracks from those of the

Short-tailed Weasel

larger Mink and Marten, which create similar patterns and are in the same family. Weasel prints can be very small, single prints generally being less than 1 inch wide. They have five toes on each foot, hind and front, but these will show only in an exceptionally clear print.

Weasel movement is typically bounding, which creates pairs or bunches of three and four prints. Since the animal is so short-legged, its body can make a connecting mark between prints in deep snow. Distance between sets of tracks depends on the speed. The straddle of Weasels is generally less than 3 inches, while that of Minks is equal to or greater than 3 inches.

VIII

Woodland Evergreen Plants

D URING THE FALL MONTHS, when summer greenery has died back and winter snows have not yet arrived, numerous small evergreen plants become conspicuous in the woods, their dark green leaves contrasting strongly with the brown leaf litter. These plants form a natural category in our winter experiences, but they represent such a wide variety of classes, orders, and families in the plant kingdom that it is difficult to generalize about them. Nonetheless, they are all hardy plants even during freezing weather, and it is worthwhile to see how most have adapted to the northern environment.

Two conditions particularly hard on plants are a lack of water during winter and a short growing season in summer. Water is unavailable to plants in winter, since it is frozen. Most of the evergreen plants have developed woody stems and waxy coatings on their leaves, both of which cut down on evaporation. Protection from drying winds is especially important, and many northern evergreen plants remain short and close to the ground, where wind speeds are substantially less.

The short growing season in the North puts limits on the amount of energy available to each plant. Many, therefore, rely more on vegetative reproduction than on reproduction by seed, since growing a flower and maturing a seed require more energy and time. Vegetative reproduction, either by underground rootstocks or trailing stems, creates small colonies of plants, a common feature among woodland evergreens.

Evergreen leaves may also aid plants during short growing seasons, for photosynthesis can continue longer into fall and start sooner in spring. They also eliminate the need for growing a whole set of new leaves each year, allowing that energy to be channeled toward reproduction.

Most plant leaves are killed by frost, for water within their cells freezes, expands, and ruptures the cell walls. Evergreen leaves are believed to overcome this handicap in at least two ways. One is to channel most of the water from within the cell walls to spaces between cells; here its expansion through freezing does less damage. Another adaptation is to increase the sugar content of the cells, thus lowering the freezing point of the remaining water.

Two other plants are included in this chapter, for they are closely related to the evergreens and also grow in woodlands. But, in total contrast to evergreens, these plants are never green; they have given up the green pigment chlorophyll and, with it, their ability to produce their own food. Instead they live in association with fungi, which dissolve organic material and make it available as nutrition for the plant. The two plants are Indian Pipes and Beechdrops. They appear more like winter weeds, but unlike the weeds, are found in the woods.

Key to Woodland Evergreen Plants

SHRUBS OVER 1 FOOT TALL

— Obvious white or brown hairs covering bottom of leaf:
  Labrador Tea and Bog Rosemary
— Sharp-pointed needlelike leaves with one side white:
  Common Juniper
— Leaves opposite or in whorls of three:
  Pale Laurel and Sheep Laurel
— Leaves 2–5 inches long bunched near end of twig; usually 6–10 feet tall, can grow much taller, found on hillsides:
  Mountain Laurel
— Leaves 1–2 inches long and pointing upward all along the stem; grows to 4 feet tall and invariably near acid bogs or cedar water streams:
  Leatherleaf

FERNS

— Leaflets undivided, rounded at their tips, and broadly attached to the stem:
  Common Polypody
— Leaflets undivided, attached at a single point to the stem:
  Christmas Fern
— Leaflets much divided, attached at a single point to the stem:
  Woodfern

TRAILING EVERGREEN VINES

— Small leaves in pairs along stem; leaves with a smooth edge and light colored midvein; red berry:
Partridgeberry
— Small leaves in pairs along stem; leaves with several rounded teeth along edge; no light midvein and no berry:
Twinflower
— Leaves in groups of threes along stem; thin thorns or bristles on stem:
Bristly Dewberry
— Large oval leaves of different sizes densely clustered on a woody trailing vine; leaves 1–5 inches long; stem often brown and hairy:
Trailing Arbutus
— Small alternate leaves on slender, hairless stems; grows mostly in acid bog habitats:
Cranberry

SMALL EVERGREEN PLANTS GROWING SINGLY OR IN GROUPS

— Light-colored veins on green leaves; leaves with a few teeth on their margins:
Spotted Pipsissewa
— Light-colored veins all over green leaves; leaves with smooth margins; grows as rosette close to ground:
Rattlesnake Plantain
— Leaves grouped in threes; leaves paper thin, and with toothed edges; golden colored rootlets; no berries:
Goldthread
— Round or oblong shiny green leaves in a rosette; plant has no main stem; leaves have long stems:
Pyrola
— A few rounded leathery leaves on each plant; leaves

smell or taste of wintergreen when crushed; leaves barely toothed on margin; frequently has red berry:
Teaberry
— Dark green, shiny, toothed leaves; leaves in whorls on the stem:
Pipsissewa

SMALL EVERGREEN PLANTS GROWING IN GROUPS WITH NEEDLELIKE OR SCALELIKE LEAVES LINING THEIR STEMS

— Clubmosses
For plants that are "nevergreens," see Beechdrops and Indian Pipes in the natural history descriptions.

Natural History Descriptions

Arbutus, Trailing (*Epigaea repens*)

Trailing Arbutus always seems luxuriant, even in winter. Its bright green leaves are the largest among our trailing evergreen plants, and their waxy edges and loose arrangement seem casual in light of winter rigors. The plant grows on rocky or sandy soil by setting down roots only in one place. Its woody stems, lined with small hairs, then trail across the rocks and grow new leaves. The roots of Arbutus are often associated with fungi that live on decaying plant matter

Trailing Arbutus

underground. The fungal roots, called "mycorrhizae," secrete enzymes that may break down the newly decaying material of rocky areas and make its nutrition available to the plant. Trailing Arbutuses are difficult to transplant or cultivate because of this association.

Arbutus is best known for its late winter and early spring flowers, which are among the most fragrant in our woods. If you find Arbutus in the fall, return there as the snow melts, and you may find the flowers already in bloom. The flowers used to be picked and sold for their fragrance, but now they are scarce because of overpicking, and are protected by law in many states.

Both the generic and species name refer to its growth habits: *Epigaea* means "on the earth" or "near the ground" and *repens* "creeping."

Beechdrops (*Epifagus virginiana*)

Beechdrops is one of the common "nevergreen" flowering plants. It rarely grows more than a foot high, and even when blooming it looks like a winter weed. This plant has no green chlorophyll, so it must get its food energy in other ways. The particular method of Beechdrops is to attach its roots to those of a green plant and live off the energy that plant produces. Beechdrops are adapted to join with the roots of only Beech trees, thus their name *Epi-*, "on," and *fagus*, "Beech." So don't bother to look for them unless you are near Beeches, or if you find Beechdrops, look up and find the tree nearby; it never fails.

Beechdrops have no leaves except for occasional scales along their stems, but they do have flowers — in fact, two

Beechdrops

kinds. The ones at the top of the stem open and are pollinated by insects in fall; they are small and often lined with fine purple stripes. The flowers at the base of the stalk are self-pollinating and never open. Both flowers produce many seeds.

Once Beechdrops become established under a Beech, they tend to continue there and form sparse colonies.

Clubmoss (*Lycopodium* species)

About 250 million years ago these small plants grew to heights of a hundred feet or more and dominated the land surfaces of the earth. Along with ferns, they were among

Lycopodium obscurum

the first land plants to develop three different organs: roots, stems, and leaves, and were also some of the first plants to develop cells that could transport water up stems for long distances. The plants that preceded them were the algae, seaweeds, and fungi, much smaller and simpler in organization.

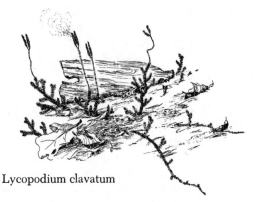

Lycopodium clavatum

For millions of years tremendous deposits of these Club-mosses accumulated on the earth's surface. They were covered over and compressed with new growth and eroded sediment. Today we dig them up as coal and burn them for heat, releasing the sun's energy they absorbed over a quarter of a billion years ago.

The Clubmosses spread by underground rootstocks, and

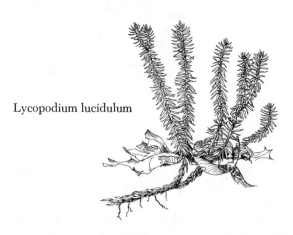

Lycopodium lucidulum

form small colonies of plants. The rootstocks differ in each species; some grow 6 inches under ground, others only an inch or two, others at the soil surface. As the rootstocks spread, the older plants die back.

Some species also reproduce by small vegetative growths that drop off their upper leaves, much like the bulbets of Wild Garlic. Clubmosses start new colonies of plants from spores, which are grown either at the base of the leaves or on long spikes called "strobili." If you knock these spikes in early winter, you can see clouds of yellow spores released into the air. The spores land on the soil and grow into a different style of plant, shaped like a minute single leaf. These are rarely found, partly because some lack chloro-

Leaves of Lycopodium complanatum

phyll and live in association with fungi underground. These small plants produce both male and female cells, which unite and grow into the Clubmosses as we see them. This life cycle is very similar to that of ferns.

Great numbers of spores are produced. They have been commercially gathered for fireworks and "flash powder" for old-time cameras. They ignite quickly and cause a small explosive flash.

Cranberry (*Vaccinium* species)

Cranberry is found in the acid soil of bogs. It is a trailing plant with shallow rootstocks that continuously send down roots and send up branches. The branches can grow to one and a half feet long and are generally low-lying. They have small, rounded, alternate evergreen leaves, and sometimes

Cranberry

bright red berries will be present along or at the tips of the stems.

There are three common varieties in our area each with a different size leaf and berry. The Small Cranberry, *Vaccinium oxycoccus,* is a very delicate plant with pointed leaves, unlike the other two species. The Large Cranberry is much larger and produces a fruit over ½ inch in diameter. Its specific Greek name, *macrocarpon,* means "large fruit." This is the variety of cranberry you buy in stores. The third variety is Mountain Cranberry, *Vaccinium vitis-idaea;* it grows only in the North or in the mountains of the mid-Atlantic states. It is midway in size between the other two and its leaves have black dots beneath.

Cranberries are a great fruit and can be gathered during fall and into winter. They are sour when eaten raw, but with cooking and sugar they make a good jam or jelly to accompany meat. Cranberries grow over much of North America but are only found locally where their habitat of acid bogs exists.

Christmas Fern (*Polystichum acrostichoides*)

Christmas fern is the largest of our evergreen ferns. It is easily recognized by the shape of its pinnae (leaflets). The

Christmas Fern

fronds lie flat on the ground in winter but are easily spotted when the snow melts because of their luxuriant dark green color. The fern is very similar to our cultivated Boston Fern, which many people keep in their houses.

Some of the fronds have smaller leaflets at their ends; these bear the fern's spores. They often die back in winter, leaving the fronds with a cut-off appearance. Christmas Fern is used in winter by florists for flower arrangements; this is probably the origin of its name — simply being used near Christmas. New fronds start growing in late winter as the snow melts.

Dewberry, Bristly (*Rubus hispidus*)

Dewberries are the trailing member of the Raspberry and Blackberry genus, *Rubus*. They are similar in appearance to

Bristly Dewberry

wild Strawberries, having three toothed leaflets joined together and, in spring, an almost identical flower. But their main difference is that Dewberry is a trailing vine; just pick up a part of the plant and you will find it connected to the other Dewberries nearby.

Dewberry typically grows in woodlands and woodland margins. It often covers a whole area, its shiny green leaves poking through the fall leaf litter. In farther northern areas it may not be evergreen, and in other areas the leaves may be green mixed with a reddish color caused by the formation of anthocyanin, the pigment present in the leaves of other evergreen plants. Small thorns or pliable bristles line its stems, and roots grow at points where erect stems and leaves emerge from the trailing vine.

Being related to the Blackberries and Raspberries, Dewberries produce a small many-seeded berry in summer. The berry is black and does not detach from the stem as do other berries. It is slightly sour, but with sugar added it can be used interchangeably in recipes calling for its sweeter cousins.

Goldthread (*Coptis groenlandica*)

Goldthread is a lovely evergreen plant with dark shiny green leaves. It loves cool climates and is often found along

Goldthread

wet mountain paths or moist shaded woods. It is easily recognized, for it has three small leaves joined together. The leaves are rounded and toothed along their edges. Our only other common evergreen with three toothed leaves is Dewberry, and that is larger and has thorns.

The common name comes from the plant's bright golden roots; by digging slightly at the base of the plant you can reveal them. The roots, when gathered and steeped in hot water, produce a bitter to stimulate the appetite or a mouthwash that may help sooth cankers and other mouth sores. It has also been called Canker Root.

Indian Pipe (*Monotropa uniflora*)

Indian Pipe is one of the two common "nevergreens," included here because they grow in the same woodlands as the evergreens, and because they are a common and puzzling sight. Indian Pipe appears as a small group of black stems four to ten inches tall, topped with urn-shaped seed

Indian Pipes

cases. The plant is a waxy white color in summer and has no leaves, except for small bracts along its stem.

In summer its white flowers droop down off the top of the stem, but as the seeds ripen in fall they turn up, as we find them in winter. The genus name means "one turn" and may refer to this turning.

Indian Pipe belongs to the same family as the evergreens Pyrola and Pipsissewa, but it has no chlorophyll — the green pigment in most other plants that enables them to manufacture food with energy from the sun. Therefore it must live off organic material, but since it can't absorb this directly, its roots associate with a fungus that can dissolve the organic matter and make it available to the plant.

There is another similar species, called Pinesap, *Monotropa hypopitys,* which has many flowers on each stem and also grows in dry woodlands. Its specific name means "under pine."

Juniper, Common (*Juniperus communis*)

Juniper is an aggressive colonizer of old fields, cutover woods, and rocky mountaintops. It is a shrub, rarely grow-

Common Juniper

ing more than 2 feet tall but spreading its tough stems to either side. Its needles grow in whorls of threes, and each has a clear white stripe on one side. They are evergreen and very sharp-pointed; they provide valuable winter cover for small animals, protecting them from both predators and weather. Deer browse the needles and birds eat the berries as well as nest in the foliage.

The berries are blue and are commercially collected both in North America and Europe for use in flavoring gin. The fruits are similar to those of Red Cedar, for the two plants are close relatives. Juniper's persistent growth on mountain slopes and old fields helps prevent erosion.

Labrador Tea (*Ledum groenlandicum*)

Labrador Tea typically grows in the cold bogs and swamps of the North. It can be easily recognized as a shrub about 2

Labrador Tea

feet tall, whose leaves have brown wool on the underside and leaf margins rolled under. The leaves are aromatic when crushed and can be gathered at any time of year for use as a tea substitute. The leaves should be dried thoroughly in the sun or near a heater before being used in tea. Bog Rosemary, *Andromeda glaucophylla*, is another small shrub often found in bogs along with Labrador Tea. It could be confused with Labrador Tea since its leaf margins are also rolled under; this similarity is important, since Bog Rosemary leaves are considered poisonous. However, Bog Rosemary leaves are very narrow, bluish-green on top, and distinctly white underneath. Also, they are not strongly aromatic, as are those of Labrador Tea.

The rolled-under, narrow, and woolly leaves of these two plants are believed to be adaptations to conserving water, for although the plants live in water, it is often too acidic for them to use, so they reduce their water needs by these adaptations.

Laurel, Mountain (*Kalmia latifolia*)

Mountain Laurel is our most luxuriant northern evergreen shrub. It can grow up to 12 feet tall and cover the understory of whole mountain hillsides. The leaves are large,

Mountain·Laurel

shiny, and dark green all through winter, forming a striking contrast with the snow-covered forest floor.

Sometimes Mountain Laurel grows in dense thickets, its twisting stems creating winter shelter for small mammals, its leaves browse for Deer. The wood is hard and fine-grained

Dried seeds of Mountain Laurel

but of such small dimension that it has been used only for small articles such as spoons and pipes. The dried flower-parts and mature seeds are clearly visible at the tips of the stems throughout winter. The leaves are often collected in winter for Christmas wreaths and decorations. In spring the plant bursts into bloom with clusters of pink blossoms.

The genus is named after Peter Kalm, a Swedish botanist and naturalist who came to America in the early 1700s. He traveled extensively in eastern North America, exploring the natural history of the land and keeping complete journals of his experiences. Linnaeus was a good friend of his and named this genus in his honor.

Laurel, Sheep (*Kalmia angustifolia*)
Pale (*Kalmia polifolia*)

The Laurel is the primary northern evergreen shrub of our woodlands. There are only three kinds in our area, one of

Sheep Laurel leaves and seeds

which, Mountain Laurel, grows tall and has large shiny leaves. It is dealt with separately above. The other two are similar in size and habitat.

Both Sheep Laurel and Pale Laurel grow to between two and three feet in height. They have narrow pale green leaves growing in whorls of three. They generally grow in small groups. The two can be easily distinguished, for Pale Laurel has two-edged twigs and produces flowers at the tips of the stems. Sheep Laurel has round twigs and produces flowers along its stems. In winter, the remains of flower parts as well as seeds may still be present on the plant.

Sheep Laurel

Laurels belong to the large family of Heaths, *Ericaceae*, which includes the Rhododendrons and a number of evergreens. The leaves are thought to be poisonous to livestock, but wild animals such as Deer and Rabbits seem unaffected by them.

Leatherleaf (*Chamaedaphne calyculata*)

Leatherleaf is the third evergreen shrub, along with Labrador Tea and Bog Rosemary, that is likely to be found at the edges of acid peat bogs. Unlike the other two it has leaf

Leatherleaf

margins that are not rolled in but flat. The leaves are broad and shiny on top and often point up along the stem. The shrub can grow to 4 feet in height but is more likely to be between 1 and 2 feet tall. In spring or even late winter, white bell-like flowers are borne along the tips of the twigs. In winter the resulting seeds are eaten by Grouse. Cottontails are known to eat the leaves. Leatherleaf is often found along with Cranberry.

Partridgeberry (*Mitchella repens*)

Partridgeberry is a very common ground cover of almost all areas. The leaves are dark green with light midveins showing through on top, and they line the trailing stems in pairs. Where leaves are produced, roots also often form if the

Partridgeberry

conditions are favorable. Partridgeberry seems to favor moist woodlands, especially under stands of White Pine.

In summer it grows paired flowers that are merged at their bases. These two flowers produce one fruit that is composed of two parts. It is red and berrylike and lasts up to a year on the vine, if not eaten by mice or grouse. The fruit is not poisonous to humans but is usually termed "barely edible," being dry and containing lots of seeds.

The common name is derived from the fact that "Partridge" or Bobwhites may eat the berries. The genus is named after John Mitchell, a man who moved to Virginia around 1725. He was most famous for his maps of the colonies, but he also had a keen interest in plants and studied them as he traveled. He often corresponded with Linnaeus about his discoveries. The specific name, *repens,* means "creeping" or "crawling."

Pipsissewa (*Chimaphila umbellata*)

Pipsissewa is a common inhabitant of the dry forest floor beneath Pines and Oaks. It appears as a group of individual plants that are usually connected by an underground root-

Pipsissewa

stock. The leaves are shiny and grow in whorls off erect stems which grow as tall as 12 inches. Some years, the plant produces a stalk protruding from its topmost whorl of leaves. This stalk divides at the top where flowers bloom in summer and seeds are matured by fall. Often these stalks and seedcases are all you will see sticking through the snow cover; dig beneath to find the evergreen plant.

Many books recommend the leaves as a pleasant trailside nibble, but anyone who has tried them knows that what little taste they have is rather unpleasant and takes effort to remove from your mouth.

Pipsissewa, Spotted (*Chimaphila maculata*)

Spotted Pipsissewa is a close relative of Pipsissewa; it differs from it by having white pigment along the veins of its dark green leaves. It is not as common as Pipsissewa but is always a prize when found. Unlike the close groups character-

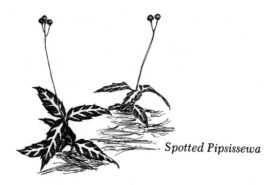

Spotted Pipsissewa

istic of Pipsissewa, Spotted Pipsissewas are more scattered, the extensive underground stems placing individual plants up to 10 feet apart. Spotted Pipsissewa also produces a flower stalk similar to that of Pipsissewa.

The common name *Pipsissewa* is believed to be of Cree Indian origin. The genus name means "winter-loving." It belongs to the Wintergreen family, *Pyrolaceae,* along with Indian Pipes and Pyrola.

Polypody, Common (*Polypodium vulgare*)

Common Polypody is undoubtedly the most hardy of the winter ferns, standing erect and green at all times. It has

Common Polypody

also been called the Rock-cap Fern because of its marvelous habit of growing on the tops of rocks. Especially in the North, where the glaciers left huge boulders, these are now often covered with a carpet of the Common Polypody. Occasionally the plant also grows on trees or logs.

The fern is easily recognized, if not by this habit, then by the way the leaflets are broadly attached to the main stem. Also the leaflets' undersides often have their large round fruit dots in two rows, easily seen and creating a strong, clear visual pattern.

The plant spreads mostly by creeping rootstocks that travel over the rock surface. These have swellings at intervals, from which the fern fronds grow. The fronds are normally about 1 foot long, new ones being produced in early summer. The plant is found worldwide in the North Temperate Zone.

Pyrola (*Pyrola* species)

Pyrola is a low-growing evergreen plant that may be partly covered by fallen tree leaves. Its leaves are generally round,

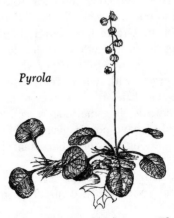

Pyrola

darker and shinier on top than underneath, and connected to a central root by a long weak reddish stem. The leaves grow as a rosette, and from its center the plant sometimes produces a tall stalk with bell-like flowers coming off its upper part.

These flower stalks may be all that first attracts you to Pyrola in winter, and you may need to clear away the snow and dead leaves to reveal the green plant. There are a number of species most easily distinguished by their flower stalks. One species, *Pyrola secunda,* has flower remains on only one side of its stalk; other species have flower remains on all sides. The common name often given to Pyrola is Shinleaf, which may be a corruption of "Shineleaf," for the upper surfaces of the leaves have a water-conserving waxy coating.

Rattlesnake Plantain (*Goddyera* species)

Rattlesnake Plantain is always exciting to find, maybe because its name suggests something unusual or dangerous. It is certainly not dangerous, but it is unusual, being small, light-colored, and usually covered by dry leaves. However, its flower stalk may be up to 20 inches high and is lined at its tip with seeds and flower remains. Rattlesnake Plantain is not related to our Common Plantain, *Plantago major,* but is a member of the Orchid family and blooms in late summer.

If you dig down through snow and leaves to the base of the flowerstalk, you will uncover the plant's rosette. Its leaves are green with white veins which must have appeared like the scales of snakeskin to early discoverers. In old-time medicine, if something resembled an affliction it was believed to have power over it; therefore, Rattlesnake Plantain was thought to help cure snakebites or scaly skin diseases.

There are four common species of *Goodyera*, each with varying numbers of white veins. The genus is named in

Rattlesnake Plantain

honor of John Goodyer, an English botanist who lived in the early 1600s.

Teaberry (*Gaultheria procumbens*)

Teaberry is a hardy little plant of the woods, a pleasure to know and find. I almost always pick a leaf or berry to chew as I pass by the plant. The bright red berries mature in fall and last all winter, but are almost always hard to see, being nestled beneath the shiny evergreen leaves.

The plant seems to thrive on acidic soil. It grows slowly by means of an underground stem, which periodically sends up small erect stems up to 6 inches tall. As with other members of the Heath family, Teaberry's leaves are well adapted for conserving moisture, their upper surface being coated with a thick waxy layer, which helps prevent evaporation and desiccation by winter winds.

Teaberry is eaten by Deer for its tasty leaves, and it is no doubt protected from extinction in late winter by suitable

Teaberry

snow cover that limits the access of Deer. Grouse and Mice may also eat the leaves or berries. The plant has long been known to contain oil of wintergreen in the leaves and berries. This is a familiar taste to us, being used in chewing gum, toothpaste, and medicines. The oil is no longer extracted from plants for commercial uses but is produced synthetically. The oil exists in Snowberry, *Gaultheria hispidula,* another plant in the same genus, but curiously it also exists in the bark of Sweet Birch, *Betula lenta,* to a greater extent than in Teaberry. The oil is tasted in Teaberry when the leaves or berries are chewed, and if equal amounts of boiling water and fresh leaves are combined and let sit for a day or two, a good tea results; just reheat the mixture. A very weak tea can be made by just steeping the fresh leaves in a teapot of hot water.

There are many common names for this plant, and each book uses a different one. I prefer Teaberry or Checkerberry, but complications arise with the name Wintergreen, for although the plant contains wintergreen oil, there is a family of plants called *Pyrolaceae,* the Wintergreen family, to which *Gaultheria* does not belong, its family being the *Ericaceae* or Heath family.

Twinflower (*Linnaea borealis*)

Twinflower is a small trailing plant partial to the cold woods of the North, but it is found south as far as Maryland and Virginia. Its paired green leaves are similar to those of Partridgeberry, but instead of being attached directly to the trailing stem, they are on short stalks that grow off the trailing stem. Twinflower is a member of the Honeysuckle family and produces two nodding pink flowers on a long stalk.

Twinflower

The famous Swedish botanist Linnaeus, who helped to stimulate great interest in collecting and naming plants in the 1700s, is often pictured with a sprig of Twinflower in his hand. The species name, *borealis*, simply means "from the north."

Woodfern (*Dryopteris* species)

The genus *Dryopteris* includes a whole group of ferns, some of which are evergreen, others only occasionally so, depending on their location. The genus name comes from two words meaning "oak" and "fern" and refers to the plants' preference for woodland habitats. Swampy lowland woods are particularly favored. Like other ferns they spread pri-

Marginal Woodfern

marily by underground rootstocks that send up new clusters of leaves at irregular intervals. At the base of these leaves in winter you will find next year's leaves already formed as tightly curled bundles. They are called fiddleheads because of their resemblance to the neck of a fiddle as they uncurl in spring. Mice use fiddleheads as an extra source of food in winter.

Two species of Woodfern are most common and prominent in the winter woods. One is Marginal Woodfern, *Dryopteris marginalis,* so named because of the placement of fruit dots on the underside margin of the leaflets. Marginal Woodfern leaves are leathery and only twice-cut: in

Leaflets and spore sacs of Spinulose Woodfern (left)
and Marginal Woodfern (right)

other words, there are leaflets and subleaflets but no further division.

The other species is called Spinulose Woodfern, *Dryopteris spinulosa*. In contrast to the above, this fern has fruit dots in from the leaflet margin and is often thrice-cut, making it appear very lacy. This fern prefers wetter areas than the ones in which Marginal Woodfern grows.

Another twice-cut Woodfern is called Goldie's Woodfern. It is similar in appearance to Marginal Woodfern but has fruit dots placed in from the leaflet margins.

Bibliography

This is only a partial list of the sources used in writing *A Guide to Nature in Winter*. The books included are those that I felt would be enjoyable, useful, and accessible to people wanting to know more.

WINTER WEEDS

Brown, Lauren. *Weeds in Winter*. W. W. Norton Co., 1976.
Fogg, John M., Jr. *Weeds of Lawn and Garden*. University of Pennsylvania Press, 1945.
Gibbons, Euell. *Stalking the Wild Asparagus*. David McKay Co., 1962.
Hall, Alan. *The Wild Food Trailguide*. Holt, Rinehart and Winston, 1973.
Martin, Alexander C., Herbert S. Zim, and Arnold L. Nelson. *American Wildlife and Plants*. Dover, 1961.
Palmer, E. Laurence. *Fieldbook of Natural History*. McGraw-Hill, 1961.
Peterson, Roger Tory, and Margaret McKenny. *A Field Guide to Wildflowers*. Houghton Mifflin, 1968.
Shosteck, Robert. *Flowers and Plants: A Lexicon*. Quadrangle, 1974.
Spencer, Edwin Rollin. *All About Weeds*. Dover, 1974.

SNOW

Bell, Corydon. *The Wonder of Snow*. Hill and Wang, 1957.
Bentley, W. A., and W. J. Humphreys. *Snow Crystals*. Dover, 1962.
Formozov, A. N. *Snow Cover as an Integral Factor of the Environment and Its Importance in the Ecology of Mammals and Birds*. Boreal Institute, University of Alberta, 1969.

LaChapelle, Edward R. *Field Guide to Snow Crystals.* University of
Washington, 1969.
Nakaya, Ukichiro. *Snow Crystals.* Harvard University Press, 1954.

WINTERING TREES

Betts, H. S. *American Woods.* U. S. Forest Service, Government Print-
ing Office, 1945–1954.
Collingwood, G. H., and Warren D. Brush. *Knowing Your Trees.* Re-
vised by Devereux Butcher. American Forestry Association, 1964.
Harlow, William M. *Trees of the Eastern United States and Canada.*
Dover, 1957.
Huntington, Annie Oakes. *Studies of Trees in Winter.* Knight and
Millet, 1902.
Peattie, Donald Culross. *A Natural History of Trees.* Houghton Mifflin,
1950.
Symonds, George W. D. *The Tree Identification Book.* M. Barrows
and Co., 1950.
Watts, Mary Theilgaard, and Tom Watts. *Winter Tree Finder.* Nature
Study Guild, 1970.
Wilson, B. F. *The Growing Tree.* University of Massachusetts, 1970.

EVIDENCE OF INSECTS

Anderson, R. F. *Forest and Shade Tree Entomology.* Wiley, 1960.
Brues, Charles T. *Insect Dietary.* Harvard University Press, 1964.
Comstock, John Henry. *An Introduction to Entomology.* Comstock Pub-
lishing Company, 1947.
Evans, Howard E. *Wasp Farm.* Anchor Press/Doubleday & Co., 1970.
Felt, Ephraim Porter. *Plant Galls and Gall Makers.* Comstock Publish-
ing Co., 1940.
Lanham, Url. *The Insects.* Columbia University Press, 1964.
Morgan, Ann Haven. *Field Book of Animals in Winter.* G. P. Putnam's
Sons, 1939.
Swain, Ralph B. *The Insect Guide.* Doubleday & Co., 1948.
Teale, Edwin Way. *Strange Lives of Familiar Insects.* Dodd, Mead &
Co., 1962.

WINTER'S BIRDS AND ABANDONED NESTS

Current information on birds is found primarily in short research
articles published in ornithological journals. The journals most useful
were:
Auk
Condor
Ibis
Wilson Bulletin

Others include:
Aviculture Magazine
Bird Banding
British Birds
Living Bird
Ornithological Monographs

MUSHROOMS IN WINTER

Boyce, John Shaw. *Forest Pathology.* McGraw-Hill, 1961.
Christensen, Clyde M. *Common Fleshy Fungi.* Burgess Publishing Co., 1967.
Krieger, Louis C. C. *The Mushroom Handbook.* Dover, 1967.
Overholts, Lee O. *Polyporaceae of the United States, Alaska, and Canada.* Revised by J. L. Lowe. University of Michigan Press, 1953.

TRACKS IN THE SNOW

Cahalane, Victor H. *Mammals of North America.* Macmillan, 1947.
Jaeger, Ellsworth. *Trails and Trailcraft.* Macmillan, 1948.
Murie, Olaus J. *A Field Guide to Animal Tracks.* Houghton Mifflin, 1954.
Palmer, Ralph S. *The Mammal Guide.* Doubleday, 1954.
Rue, Leonard Lee, III. *Sportsman's Guide to Game Animals.* Outdoor Life Books, 1968.
Seton, Ernest Thompson. *Animal Tracks and Hunter Signs.* Doubleday, 1958.

The most current information on mammals exists as short articles in two leading wildlife journals:
Journal of Mammalogy
Journal of Wildlife Management

WOODLAND EVERGREEN PLANTS

Clute, Willard Nelson. *Our Ferns: Their Haunts, Habits, and Folklore.* Frederick A. Stokes Co., 1938.
Cobb, Boughton. *A Field Guide to Ferns.* Houghton Mifflin, 1956.
Cunningham, James, A., and John E. Klimas. *Wildflowers of Eastern American.* Knopf, 1974.
Gibbons, Euell. *Stalking the Healthful Herbs.* David McKay Co., 1966.
Milne, Lorus, and Margery Milne. *Living Plants of the World.* Random House, 1967.
Symonds, George W. D. *The Shrub Identification Book.* William Morrow & Co., 1963.

Index

A Guide to Nature in Winter is an un-paralleled introduction to the wintertime natural world. Nature is never dormant: on close observation, a silent, snow-blanketed winter landscape reveals itself as the setting for intense and purposeful activity in the plant and animal worlds. Because natural activity is greatly simpli-fied in winter, though, it is the ideal season to introduce oneself to the complex series of relationships that tie the natural world together.

Perhaps this volume is better described as eight comprehensive field guides in one. Donald Stokes covers thoroughly the eight prominent aspects of winter most easily studied in the field: winter weeds, snow crystals, wintering trees, evidence of in-sects, birds and abandoned nests, winter mushrooms, tracks in the snow, and ever-green plants. For each topic, he provides a general introduction, a key to field identi-fication of items within the topic, and a natural history description of each item (arranged alphabetically, by common name).

The 485 stunning pen-and-ink drawings that grace these pages make accurate field identification easy and convey a feeling